DISCOVERING HISTORIC

C000001145

SCOTLAND'S WARS AND WARRIORS

WINNING AGAINST THE ODDS

DAVID H CALDWELL

SERIES EDITOR: ALEXANDRA SHEPHERD

HISTORIC SCOTLAND

EDINBURGH: THE STATIONERY OFFICE

About the Author

David H Caldwell was brought up in Ardrossan, on the Firth of Clyde, and graduated with a degree in archaeology from Edinburgh University in 1973. He joined the then National Museum of Antiquities of Scotland that year and has continued to work for the National Museums of Scotland, currently as the curator of the Scottish Medieval Collections. He was awarded a doctorate by Edinburgh University in 1982 for a study of the early use of guns in Scotland and has published extensively, including works on Scottish weapons and warfare. He has directed excavations at Eyemouth Fort, Berwickshire, Auldhill, Ayrshire, and at Finlaggan on Islay, the centre of the Lordship of the Isles. He is married, has three children, and now lives in Fife.

Acknowledgements

The author is very grateful to the many friends and colleagues who, over the years, have provided him with help and information. A particular debt is owed to Stuart Maxwell who first encouraged him to take up an interest in Scottish weapons and taught him much of what he knows. This book would be very much poorer but for the unstinting efforts of the editor, Alexandra Shepherd, in improving the text and providing many of the illustrations. Grateful thanks are also due for illustrations to Mark Dennis, the United Distillers' Company, Lord Egremont, Fraser Hunter, Richard Oram, Leonie Paterson and Ian Shepherd, and to Historic Scotland and the National Museums of Scotland.

For Helen, Barbara and Michael

Cover illustrations show *front*: William Wallace, a statue of 1888 (W Grant Stevenson) in Aberdeen (Ian Shepherd) and Mons Meg, the great gun in Edinburgh Castle (Historic Scotland); *back*: Dunadd, Argyll, stronghold of the Gaels of Dal Riata (Historic Scotland) and a reconstruction of the siege of Tantallon, East Lothian, in 1528 (Historic Scotland).

Published by The Stationery Office and available from:
The Stationery Office Bookshops
71 Lothian Road, Edinburgh EH3 9AZ (counter service only)
123 Kingsway, London WC2B 6PQ
68-69 Bull Street, Birmingham B4 6AD Tel 0121-236 9696 Fax 0121-236 9699
33 Wine Street, Bristol BS1 2BQ Tel 0117-926 4306 Fax 0117-929 4515
9-21 Princes Street, Manchester M60 8AS Tel 0161-834 7201 Fax 0161-833 0634
16 Arthur Street, Belfast BT1 4GD Tel 01232 238451 Fax 01232 235401
The Stationery Office Oriel Bookshop
The Friary, Cardiff CF1 4AA
Tel 01222 395548 Fax 01222 384347

The Stationery Office publications are also available from:
The Publications Centre (mail, telephone and fax orders only)
PO Box 276 London SW8 5DT
General enquiries 0171-873 0011
Telephone orders 0171-873 9090
Fax orders 0171-873 8200

Accredited Agents
(see Yellow Pages) and through good booksellers

First published 1998 by The Stationery Office Limited, South Gyle Crescent, Edinburgh, EH12 9EB.

ISBN 0 11 495786 X

British Library Cataloguing in Publication Data
A catalogue record for this book is available from the British Library

Applications for reproduction should be made to The Stationery Office Limited

CONTENTS

FOREWORD

Scotland is a country where the imprint of history is still clearly visible in the landscape, in its houses, churches, farmsteads and settlements large and small. All these have coloured, and been coloured by, their setting in mountains or moorland, on fertile pasture or sandy shore, at loch-side or rivermouth. Of paramount importance has always been the all-encompassing influence of the sea for Scotland is set amidst the searoads of the Celtic provinces in the west and the Scandinavian regions to the north, the trading routes with the mainland of Europe to the east and the land and sea approaches to that dominant neighbour, England, in the south. Scotland's cultural history has thus been moulded by a mixture of influences, fluctuating in importance, absorbed and transformed in ways that are peculiarly Scottish. This series aims to provide a view across the mosaic of that history from its earliest beginnings to the present day; each volume covers one individual aspect of the panorama but the themes are interwoven: kings and queens, heraldry and houses, wars and warriors, stained glass and churches - all link to create a tapestry of Scotland's vigorous past and her historic present.

The image of the Scottish soldier is a popular one in folk song and story, book and film. Some of Scotland's battles are among the most famous in history, often presented as more romantic than the reality is likely to have been, yet giving that sense of fighting against the odds that is so much a part of Scotland's past. This volume looks at that reality, from the earliest warriors, their strongholds and weaponry, through the development of systems of mounted knights and yeoman foot-soldiers to the ultimate transformation of Highland clansmen into professional soldiers in a British army. The detail of battle plans, campaigns, organisation and equipment bring into sharp focus a text that follows the history of Scotland's wars and warriors for more than fifteen hundred years.

ALEXANDRA SHEPHERD
Series Editor

CHAPTER 1

EARLY ORIGINS OF A WARRING NATION

T his book is about Scottish warfare. The main emphasis is on war at an international level, primarily with England. It looks at how Scotland survived as a separate kingdom, and how her people's military skills were chanelled after union with England.

It is no mere catalogue of battles, and indeed the reader will look in vain for even a mention of, for example, Culblean in 1335, Harlaw in 1411, Preston in 1648 or Falkirk in 1746. Battles were often mistakes. The Scots were usually more successful when they avoided them. Nor is this a work just about famous men. Scotland was not over-endowed with great military leaders, producing only one of undoubted world class stature in the person of Robert Bruce. Rather it is about a whole nation of warriors. Perhaps a dogged determination to win through despite the setbacks was embued in the whole Scottish population and was their ultimate military strength.

Generations of Scots have been inured to war and it is no surprise that many see Scotland as a country of warriors. How this fighting spirit was tapped in the years after union with England is also considered in this book, although the Scottish part in the building of the British Empire and in the great wars of this century are only touched on lightly. These matters, like individual regimental histories, would need whole volumes of their own to do them proper justice.

THE EARLIEST WARFARE

The land which is now Scotland has been populated for the last 10,000 years. The earliest occupants were hunters and gatherers. They had bows and arrows, spears and harpoons for killing animals. It is only from the later third millennium BC, at a time when people were more settled, and farming and stock-raising had long been practised, that there is evidence of weapons specifically designed for fighting. They are of bronze, at first just daggers, but, by about 1200 BC, swords as well, and new research has shown that they often have nicks or dents along their edges, caused by striking other blades.

While daggers may be interpreted as weapons for self-defence, swords, shields and spears conjure up an image of a society in which warfare, or the threat of it, played a significant part. Archaeologists have now dated early occupation of defended hill-top settlements or hill forts to a few centuries BC. Some with stone ramparts interlaced with timbers were destroyed by fire, the heat from the flames causing the stonework to *vitrify* - turn to a hard glass-like substance. There is controversy over exactly how this was achieved, and in many cases when, but it is surely indicative of conflict.

Early swords, of types common in the period 1000-750 BC. They come from as far apart as Ness on the Isle of Lewis and Mey in Caithness (National Museums of Scotland).

Certainly, by the time of the first Roman intervention in Scotland, about AD 80, the countryside was covered with a rash of forts and other defended settlements, and we know from the descriptions of classical writers that we are dealing with at least 16 tribal groups on the Scottish mainland.

THE BATTLES WITH ROME

The earliest record of warfare in Scotland is in AD 84 or 85 when the Roman army under Agricola encountered and beat a confederation of northern tribes - the Caledonians - led by Calgacus, at Mons Graupius. The identification of the battlefield has been one of the great challenges of Roman archaeology. Currently many favour the area of the camp at Durno, just to the north-east of Bennachie, a prominent hill in Aberdeenshire.

If this battle really took place in the way described by the Roman historian Tacitus (who was actually Agricola's son-in-law), then Mons Graupius is likely to have been the biggest battle on Scottish soil until that time. It is always legitimate to question or doubt our sources

Tap o'Noth hillfort, Rhynie, Grampian. The fort is sited on a summit at 563m (1850 ft) above sea level. The massive stone wall enclosing the summit has been vitrified - turned to a hard glass-like substance - as a result of the high temperatures reached when its timberwork was fired (Ian Shepherd).

The great fortress of Bennachie, in whose shadow the battle of Mons Graupius may have been fought, where the Romans defeated the Caledonians in AD 84 or 85 (Ian Shepherd).

After Mons Graupius: Caledonians and Romans lie dead and wounded at this reconstruction of the battle for the Archaeolink prehistory park, Oyne, Aberdeenshire (Ian Shepherd).

when it comes to military history. So much is at stake in warfare - and also confused. Good propaganda was of the utmost importance. In the case of Mons Graupius, Agricola desperately needed a major victory as a career move, and was fortunate to have a compliant Tacitus to make it history. Tacitus was even able to give appropriate pre-battle speeches by the opposing commanders. It is well to remember that the defeated Caledonians have left us no records at all.

Tacitus' readers were meant to admire Agricola's skill and judgement in attacking a strongly positioned enemy army and the steadfastness of his men in comprehensively defeating their opponents. The Caledonians are said to have been drawn up, 30,000 strong - no doubt an exaggeration - at the base of Mons Graupius. They were armed with throwing spears, long swords for slashing, and shields, and had a force of chariots but these were no match for the disciplined Roman cavalry. The Romans mounted a full frontal attack on the Caledonian lines and soon pushed their front line back. Agricola anticipated an attempt by their rear lines to encircle his army by sending in his cavalry to scatter them as they streamed forward. Soon the whole Caledonian army was in flight, pursued by the enemy cavalry.

A section of the Antonine Wall, the most northerly Roman frontier defence wall, at Croy Hill near Glasgow (Historic Scotland).

OPPOSITE: *Traprain Law, East Lothian, a stronghold of the people known to the Romans as the Votadini, and in their own language as the Gododdin. The stronghold would have dominated the East Lothian countryside as it still does today (Fraser Hunter).*

However, from this the Caledonians obviously learnt the folly of bringing a well trained and supplied imperial army into battle, and the Romans were unable to record any other resounding wins in their dealings

The Roman occupation of Scotland

THE ROMAN FRONTIER

The Roman general Agricola hoped to conquer all of Britain, but he was recalled in AD 83 and the Emperor Hadrian abandoned all of Scotland, building a stone wall across the country from the Tyne to the Solway Firth. Work started around AD 122. It was garrisoned by troops based in forts and fortlets at regular intervals along its length. Hadrian's successor, Antoninus Pius, built another wall, the Antonine Wall, begun about AD 142. Constructed of turf, with a flanking ditch, it spanned the country from the Forth to the Clyde and was well supported by forts and a system of roads. It was Imperial Rome's most northerly frontier - but not for long: by the 160s AD this was re-established on Hadrian's Wall.

with the tribes of the north. They failed or declined to encompass the whole of Britain in their empire, and their response to raids by Calgacus' successors was the erection of walls and forts, and punitive

expeditions. Their inability to create a secure northern frontier in Britain was to be one of the major causes of the collapse of Roman Britain in the early 5th century.

DARK AGE CONFLICT

Pictish cross-slab at Aberlemno in Angus. The back of the cross-slab has warriors, some on foot, some on horseback, in three tiers. Those on the left-hand side can be interpreted as the victorious Picts. Infantrymen resolutely stand their ground with spear, sword and shields against a mounted attack, while at the top a cavalryman pursues a defeated opponent who has already thrown down his shield. Only the supposed Angles on the right wear helmets (Historic Scotland).

Viewed from a distance of several hundred years, the period between the Romans and the emergence of a powerful and stable Kingdom of the Scots by the early 11th century, seems a time of constant struggle, as different peoples strove for supremacy. The Picts in the north, and Britons in the south, were the descendants of the tribes encountered by the Romans. They were joined by Angles pushing up from the south, Scandinavians, and Gaels (the *Scotti*) from Ireland.

The paltry sources for these times have left us names of battles, but little to inform us about strategy and tactics. Armies, or war-bands, were probably often only a few hundred strong, and were of no account unless led by a king or noble who could command respect for his prowess. The heroic nature of this warfare is brought out in an early poem written by Aneirin in the Cumbric (Welsh) language of the Britons. *The Gododdin* is about the band of 300 chosen warriors

feasted by King Mynyddog of the Gododdin, who held the Lothians, in Din Eidyn (Edinburgh) for a whole year before it went south against the heathen Angles. In the battle at Catterick around AD 600, the Gododdin army was annihilated, only Aneirin escaping to tell the tale. Regrettably the poem is only the first of many examples in Scottish history of an obsessive fascination with failure.

Dunnichen, near Forfar, the site of the battle of Nechtansmere in AD 685 where the Pictish king, Brude, won a decisive victory over the Anglian king, Egfrith (Historic Scotland).

The poem lists the qualities of our heroes. All of them rode to battle and some of them fought on horseback. They wore protective armour, sometimes described as mail-coats, but there is no mention of helmets. They were armed with shields, swords and various types of spears, including ones for throwing. For graphic images of such warriors we can turn to the sculptured stones of the neighbouring Picts. One in particular, a cross-slab at Aberlemno in Angus, is believed by some to be a representation of an actual battle, in this case fought at nearby Nechtansmere (Dunnichen Moss) in 685. Here the Picts won a resounding victory over Egfrith, the Anglian king of Northumbria, who was slain with many of his men.

A surprising omission from this slab and other early carvings is evidence for the use of the bow and arrow in warfare. Projectile points recovered from some forts of the period, for instance the early Scottish stronghold of Dunadd in Argyll, may be for use as spear-points and javelin-heads rather than arrows. There is, however, some evidence for the use of crossbows, although not in battle. They are shown in hunting scenes on some Pictish stones, for example the 'Drosten Stone' at St Vigean's in Angus, which may date to the 9th

A detail from 'the Drosten Stone', a Pictish sculpture of the 9th century at St Vigeans in Angus, showing a man firing a crossbow (Historic Scotland).

century. There is also an antler nut, part of the firing mechanism for a crossbow, from a crannog (an artifical island dwelling) at Buiston in Ayrshire, occupied in the Early Christian period.

The Viking Scandinavians appeared relatively late on the scene, initially around AD 800 as pirates terrorising the north and west: Iona was first attacked in 795 and in 870 they took Dumbarton Rock, the capital of the Britons. Twenty years or so later they captured the great east coast fortress of Dunnottar, just to the south of Stonehaven, and in the early years of the 10th century the important inland centres, Dunkeld and Dunblane were plundered. But warfare gave way to settlement: the Western Isles remained under Norse control until 1266, and Orkney and Shetland were only ceded in 1468-69 when James III married Margaret of Denmark. Norse earls and kings were a real threat to mainland Scotland down to the 13th century. At that time Norse people and their traditions were finally assimilated into the greater Scottish cultural melting-pot. Their legacies of seafaring and fighting were to be influential in the west for many centuries.

Antler crossbow nut, preserved from Buiston crannog Ayrshire (an Early Historic settlement on an artificial island) (National Museums of Scotland).

A Viking long ship, carved on a Scandinavian-style cross at Iona, dating to the 10th century. The figures in the boat appear to be wielding weapons (Shepherd).

It is to the Gaels (Scots) that particular attention has to be paid as the ultimate winners, and also because their military system is remarkably well documented by comparison with their neighbours. The Scots had been settling in south-west Scotland since at least the 5th century. About 500, Fergus Mor mac Eirc, king of the Dal Riata in Northern Ireland, came to rule in Argyll. Until the early 7th century his descendants continued to hold on to land in Ulster, but the future of Dal Riata lay in North Britain.

THE ARMY OF THE GAELS

A history of the men of Scotland (the *Senchus Fer nAlban*) originally composed in the 7th century, contains information on how the Gaels of Dal Riata were organised for warfare. Their society was tribal, with several ranks of nobility and freemen distinguishable from the mass of commoners. Only the houses of freemen and nobles were assessed for naval and military service, and for this purpose the houses were grouped into units of 20, each of which supplied 28 men.

This ratio of 28 men per 20 houses was to enable two ships to be supplied by each unit of houses. The ships had 14 oarsmen, seven aside. They were of *curach* (coracle) construction, with a wooden frame covered with leather, and had sails. They were not just for transporting men but could be used in battle, as in 719 when there was civil war in Dal Riata, the Cenel Loairn fighting the Cenel nGabrain in the earliest recorded sea-battle in the British Isles. These ships were to be superseded by the clinker-built, wooden long-ships of the Norsemen.

SEA POWER

The importance of ships in warfare goes back a long way. Agricola relied on a fleet for provisioning his army when campaigning in Scotland in the AD 80s, and Aedan, King of Dal Riata, had a sufficient fleet in the 580s to allow him to raid Orkney and Man. The Picts are also known to have been a sea-power, 150 of their ships being wrecked in AD 729, but it is the Norse people who settled in Scotland from the 9th century who left the most enduring maritime legacy. Their ships were probably technically superior to those of the Picts and the Scots. More significantly, they had the skill and confidence to undertake long sea voyages under sail, and fight naval engagements from them.

There were three chief peoples in the kingdom of Dal Riata in the 7th century. When the king required a hosting (*Slogad*) the 430 houses of the Cenel nOengusa in Islay could be expected to supply 600 men, the 420 houses of the Cenel Loairn in Lorn a further 600 men, and the 560 houses of the Cenel nGabrain in Kintyre and Cowal, 800 men.

This army of 2,000 men was a sizeable one for its time. That it had some command structure is hinted at by an emphasis on units of a hundred. It is impossible to say how different the Gaels' system of military service was from their neighbours. Was it more flexible and reliable? Did it produce armies with more backbone than the typical warband of the period? We will never know. It served the Gaels of Dal Riata well, and in a modified way remained the method of raising an army for the early kingdom of the Scots.

WITH GOD ON THEIR SIDE

The Monymusk Reliquary, a house-shaped shrine of c. 700. Many scholars believe this is the Brecbennoch of St Columba, carried into battle before the Scottish Army (National Museums of Scotland).

Another possible advantage the early Scots had in warfare was the support of a strong missionary church. Indeed the great 6th-century saint, Columba, based on the island of Iona, was warlike in attitude and positively interested in battle. Contemporaries believed he could successfully intercede with God for victory in battle for those he favoured. After his death kings and warlords prayed for his help. His crozier, carried before the Scottish army, brought success in battle, as

in 904 when a Norse army from Dublin was defeated in Strathearn and their king, Ivar II killed. From the late 12th century there is evidence of the carrying of another Columban relic into battle. This was the Brecbennoch, thought by many to be a little-house shrine rediscovered at Monymusk House, Aberdeenshire, in the 19th century. The Brecbennoch was in the keeping of Arbroath Abbey and must surely have been with the patriotic abbot, Bernard of Linton, at the Battle of Bannockburn in 1314.

Dunadd, Argyll, a royal centre of the Gaels of Dal Riata (Historic Scotland).

Whatever their inspiration, it was largely success in war which led to the dominance of the Scots in North Britain. In 843 Kenneth MacAlpin of Dal Riata became king of Pictland, an extensive territory spanning the country from Fife to the far north. Under his descendants the new combined kingdom of Gaels and Picts was to go from strength to strength, at first known as Alba, and, from the 11th century, as the Kingdom of the Scots. It was one of the great success stories of the early medieval world, a political and military power to be reckoned with, richly endowed with its own cultural and artistic traditions.

CHAPTER 2

THE RISE AND FALL OF THE KNIGHTS

FORTUNES OF WAR IN THE 12TH AND 13TH CENTURIES

In the 12th century Scotland became part of a wider European world. Sweeping changes in many areas of life and culture resulted from the deliberate policies of her kings, who saw themselves as part of an international Anglo-Norman elite; for, despite their birthright, they had mixed freely in English ruling circles and were also major landholders in that country.

From the reign of David I, Anglo-Normans, Flemings and others were encouraged to come and settle in Scotland, and were the main instrument of initiating new practices. The institutions of government and the Church were reformed; great stone churches were erected and burghs founded as centres of trade and commerce; the first Scottish coins were minted, and a whole range of new items of daily use made their appearance.

The new Anglo-Norman landholders saw themselves first and foremost as a warrior caste, based in castles which they themselves first built in Scotland. The introduction of knights has been considered one of the most momentous developments in European warfare. In Scotland we have not only to consider the impact of knights in warfare but also their effectiveness alongside the traditional Scottish fighting forces.

OPPOSITE: *Knights in action from a facsimile of the 11th-century Bayeux tapestry. Although produced in France and depicting a Saxon-Norman conflict, the images are equally representative of Scottish knights of the time.*

King David I, and his grandson, Malcolm IV, from a 19th-century facsimile of Malcolm's 1159 charter to Kelso Abbey. Despite their Celtic heritage David and his successors were respected leaders of Anglo-Norman society.

KNIGHT SERVICE

Knights were heavily armoured cavalry. Strictly speaking, not all heavily armoured cavalry were knights. Knighthood was an honour that had to be aspired to, but it is usual to refer to the cavalry collectively as 'knights'. Some early Scottish knights have left striking images of themselves on their seals. They were clothed in a hauberk - a coat of mail extending to the knees with a hood to cover the head. Over this was worn a conical iron helmet with a protective nasal piece, and a large triangular shield was carried on the left forearm for warding off blows. These shields were often decorated, and by the 1170s a formalised system of heraldry had been developed so that opponents on the battlefield could be recognised by the designs on their shields.

A 12th-century seal found at Raewick, Shetland, now in the National Museums of Scotland. It depicts a knight on horseback wearing a hauberk of mail, and armed with a sword and a shield with a large boss (National Museums of Scotland).

The two principal weapons were a spear, gripped firmly between arm and body, and a double-edged sword, more suitable for cutting strokes than for stabbing. These remained the essential pieces of arms and armour into the early 14th century, though the appearance of the individual items changes as a matter of fashion. In the case of helmets there was a real improvement in their design by the beginning of the 13th century with pot-shaped forms, completely enveloping the head. Iron reinforcing plates or corsets of plates were also making their appearance.

Perhaps the most important item of knightly equipment was the horse. These were no ordinary farm animals or beasts of burden, but large, sturdy animals, capable of carrying an armoured man at the gallop, and from the mid 13th century their own armour of mail or leather and quilting as well. When King Alexander I, early in the 12th century, wished that his munificence to St Andrews Cathedral should be remembered, he had his Arab steed presented at the altar. There were few personal possessions in Scotland at that time more valuable than such a horse.

Attention must be drawn to one last piece of knightly equipment, the humble stirrup. Stirrups gave the knights that security of position to stay astride their galloping horses and to withstand the shock of battle.

MacBeth had a force of Norman knights, all killed in battle against Siward, Earl of Northumbria, in 1054. Both Duncan II and King Edgar had English and French knights in the 1090s to assist them in gaining the Scottish throne, but it was only with the reign of their younger brother David from 1124 that there is undoubted evidence for a royal policy of establishing a Scottish force of knights.

Knights were very expensive because they required years of training and costly equipment. They were, therefore, territorially based. Grants of land were given in return for the service of knights in warfare. Most of these grants were made to newcomers, mostly of Anglo-Norman or Flemish origin, many of whom came from families already settled in England, often on estates held there by the Scottish kings. A few of the more important or favoured of these were given large estates in return for the service of several knights. Thus Robert de Brus, ancestor of King Robert Bruce, held land in Annandale of King William I for the service of ten knights.

Much more typical were the lesser men who were given estates for the service of one knight – themselves. Such a one was Alexander de Saint Martin, granted the lands of Alstaneford in East Lothian by King David I for the service of half a knight. He was to be paid ten merks of silver yearly until the grant was made up to a full knight's fee. Presumably in the interim he was only required to do service for half the time or without the full knightly equipment or retinue.

In other cases a serjeant, or mounted man less completely armed than a knight, may have been provided, or an archer. This so-called 'free service' was a serious obligation on the landholders in question. They were truly professional soldiers, but probably never numbered more than a few hundred.

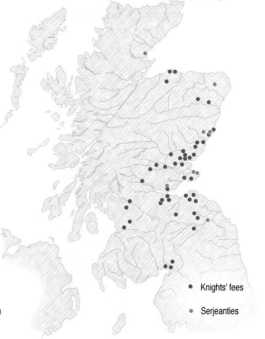

Distribution map of lands known to have been held for the service of knights or serjeants by 1214. They are concentrated in the fertile Eastern Lowlands where the royal authority was strongest (after G C Simpson & B Webster).

● Knights' fees

● Serjeanties

A NETWORK OF CASTLES

SIEGEWORK

The reliance on castles inevitably meant the development of ways to capture them. In 1174 King William the Lion had a stone-throwing machine, probably a large catapult, at the siege of Wark Castle on the Border with England. Possibly it was supplied by his Flemish mercenaries, but in this case was not successful. The first stone it cast hardly left the sling, striking one of the Scottish knights to the ground, though not killing him! Other military engines ('machines') are mentioned in the 1260s. It is only with the English occupation at the end of the 13th and beginning of the 14th centuries that there is much evidence for siegecraft. The English used a variety of military machines in Scotland, including ones which fired missiles, and towers which could be wheeled alongside walls.

Intimately linked with the new warrior aristocracy were castles. Twelfth-century Scottish kings obviously intended that the country should be covered by a network of castles. They could make secure centres of local administration and be a protection against invaders. Typically sheriffs, royal officials based in the localities, operated from castles built alongside burghs, and in 1263, in the time of the Norwegian invasion, we find 120 serjeants had to be hired to keep the castle of Ayr against an expected attack from King Haakon of Norway.

Almost all of these early castles were built of earth and timber. Exceptionally at Edinburgh and Roxburgh there may have been large stone keeps like those erected in England. Typically there was a motte, a large earthen mound, fortified in timber round the top, often with an adjacent fortified bailey or enclosure. The mottes vary greatly in size and height, and excavation has demonstrated that some were crowned with a wooden tower, like Barton Hill, Perthshire and Keir Knowe of Drum in Stirlingshire. Others like Castlehill of Strachan, Kincardineshire, had a hall.

There were large areas of the country, for instance the Lordship of Galloway, where royal authority was weak or openly challenged, and the establishment of castles of new Anglo-Norman and Flemish overlords was seen as a means of holding down the country. There are some 40 mottes in Wigtonshire and the Stewartry of Kirkcudbright,

Duffus Castle, Moray: a large motte-and-bailey castle erected in the 12th century by Freskin, an ancestor of the Murrays. The timberworks were replaced in stone about 1300 (Ian Shepherd).

24

many no doubt the newly erected castles of the 'English' who were slaughtered or ejected in a revolt in 1174. A group of mottes in Upper Clydesdale may be associated with a colony of landlords, mostly Flemish, settled here in the 12th century. Fourteenth-century documentation indicates that the owners of these mottes owed castle-ward at the royal castle at Lanark - that is, served in its garrison when required.

Very little is known of the residences of Scottish kings or nobles prior to the 12th century, but there is no evidence that they were strongly fortified. Royal palaces at Scone and Dunfermline did not develop into medieval castles and other early royal forts like Dumbarton and Edinburgh may have temporarily lost their role as strongholds. Edinburgh makes a reappearance as a royal stronghold from 1193, when St Margaret died there shortly after the news of the death of her husband Malcolm Canmore and son Edward on a raid into England. Stirling Castle, on a rock remarkably similar to Edinburgh, was a residence of Alexander I in the early 12th century, the place where he died in 1124. As the century wore on more and more royal castles are recorded, many like Dumfries, Perth and Selkirk adjacent to royal burghs.

Distribution of mottes in Scotland (after G Stell).

Increasingly in the 13th century, the king and the great families built castles of stone. Some were simple stone enclosures with buildings ranged along the walls, including the royal castles at Tarbert in Argyll and Kincardine (Kincardineshire), perhaps both the work of King Alexander II. Later in the century were built some truly impressive stone castles with projecting corner towers to provide flanking fire with crossbows and bows, twin-towered gatehouses and large donjon towers for the extra security of the castellan. The best surviving example is at

Kildrummy Castle, Aberdeenshire, the chief castle of the Earls of Mar. The top of the shield-shaped castle rests on the edge of a steep ravine and the rest is surrounded by a large ditch. Its curtain wall has four projecting towers and a twin-towered gatehouse with drawbridge. One round tower, adjacent to the ravine, acted a the donjon, a strongpoint where a last stand might be made when the rest of the castle had fallen. Within the curtain walls are other buildings, including a chapel and the great hall. Construction began in the early 13th century, but its final form may not have been achieved until 1290. The English may have added the gatehouse when they captured the castle in 1306 (Historic Scotland).

Kildrummy in Aberdeenshire although there were equally large and impressive castles built by the Stewarts at Dundonald in Ayrshire and by Walter de Moravia at Bothwell in the Clyde Valley, and several smaller stone castles of great strength including Caerlaverock in Dumfries and Inverlochy at Fort William.

SCOTTISH SERVICE

Early grants of land often mention the obligation on the landholder to perform forinsec or Scottish service. The terminology is new but this was the same requirement as in earlier times to do military service when required by the king. This Scottish service was clearly different from knight service, placing no emphasis on training or equipment, but primarily requiring quotas of men for the army or host in time of war. It was to remain the basis of Scotland's military might down to the 17th century.

In the 12th and 13th centuries there was an understanding of how many men were required from each unit of land. For instance, in much of the country the basic agricultural unit was the davach, not a particular size of property, but one which paid certain dues and rents. Each davach provided 20 men for the army, or in some coastal and island locations in the west a galley of 20 oars. Landholders who owed knight service were expected to provide Scottish service as well.

In the later medieval period it was understood that the host could be called out for a maximum of 40 days in any one year, and this may also have been the norm at this time. Its commander-in-chief was usually the king, while leadership of its various units was naturally provided by the nobles and other great landholders. The earls had had

Battle axe of typical 13th-century type (Shepherd).

a particular responsibility for calling out and leading contingents of men from their own earldoms, but this task might also be undertaken by the sheriffs.

The full size of the Scottish host at this time can only be guessed at. Numbers are given by more than one early chronicler, but by comparison with more credible figures for later armies can readily be dismissed as exaggerations. Perhaps a maximum of 10,000 men would not be a bad guess.

Their weapons are more reliably described. For instance the English chronicler, Mathew Paris, describes the Scottish foot soldiers in 1244 as being lightly armed and fittingly supplied with axes, spears and bows. In fact many Scots notoriously went into battle with little clothing at all. Thus at the Battle of the Standard in 1138 they are described as naked, 'worthless Scots with half-bare buttocks'. It is evident that in the 12th century their spears included a type of javelin which was thrown at the enemy. Axes are particularly noted as their weapon together with bows in a Scandinavian source for the Battle of Largs in 1263.

THE FAILURE OF THE KNIGHTS?

The earth and timber castles associated with the new military order could not have been an effective obstacle for a determined foe, but there is little evidence of the great stone castles being seriously threatened before the arrival of Edward I of England with his siege machines at the beginning of the 14th century. Despite, however, the importance attached by early Scottish kings to their knights, and the prominence they achieved in early documents, their effectiveness in warfare has to be questioned. An easy problem to identify is that there

were not enough of them to be matched against the English, but whether in large or small engagements, it is difficult to identify occasions when their presence was crucial to Scottish strategy, and more importantly to its success.

At the Battle of the Standard in 1138 when David I's expansionist ambitions in England received a momentary check, the king kept his knights in reserve and had his Galwegian foot soldiers spearhead his attack with disastrous results. It was the stone throwing, axe-wielding Scottish foot who saw off King Haakon's Norwegians at Largs in 1263. The only contribution noted for the knights was a vainglorious ride by one through the Norwegian ranks which cost him his life.

David I's father, Malcolm III, had been able to terrorise the north of England as far as Durham. An English commentator claimed that, after a particularly devastating raid in 1070, Scotland was so filled with slaves and handmaids of the English race that not a hamlet or even a hut could be found without them. It was the descendants of Malcolm's warriors who underpinned the successes of David I. English chroniclers contrast the noble and chivalrous Scottish kings with their people, described in one source as 'barbarous and unclean,

The monument at Largs, Ayrshire, commemorating the victory of the Scots in 1263 over the Norwegians. As a result of this battle the Scots regained the Western Isles (Caldwell).

The Vikings at Largs: represented in stained glass by Sir James Guthrie at Knockderry Castle, Argyllshire, 1887 (Michael Donnelly).

KING·HACO·OF·NORWAY·BEFORE·THE·BATTLE·OF·LARGS

neither subdued by bitter cold nor stunted by severe hunger, and they rely upon swift feet and light armour. They regard as nothing the dread close of bitter death among the members of their own family, but amongst strangers they surpass all in cruelty '.

Thanks to men like these, when David I died in 1153, he held all of England to the Tyne and Ribble. In the reign of his grandson, William I, royal power was consolidated in Galloway, the north and the west. In the 13th century the Isle of Man and all the Hebrides were won from the Norse.

While accepting that it is the paucity of surviving documentation as much as anything which allows us to downplay the contribution of the knights, as we will show below, the future of Scottish arms lay with the host. This, however, was only after the opening campaign in the Wars of Independence, in 1296, when the English king, Edward I, had decided to wrest control of Scotland from King John Balliol.

As Edward I headed north with his army towards Berwick the Scots raided into Cumberland, hoping, without success, to distract him. Instead he readily took Berwick by storm and slaughtered all its inhabitants. The only response by the leaders of the Scottish army was to set out on a strategically futile revenge raid into Tynedale and Redesdale.

Meanwhile Edward had sent on part of his army to besiege Dunbar Castle. The returning Scots now decided on more direct action and thought to relieve the siege of the castle. In the absence of their king their army was commanded by a group of the nobles. Their march to Dunbar was not unobserved and they were opposed by an advance guard of the English under the Earl Warenne. It would appear that the engagement was essentially a cavalry one. The Scottish horse probably numbered rather more than the English, but was unequal to the task. Lighter and less experienced it was readily dispersed in an ill-judged charge. Some of it was chased several miles from the battlefield. Many sought refuge in Dunbar Castle, while the Scottish foot, left leaderless, was severely handled by the jubilant English. The Scottish knights had wasted their one great chance of military glory and left their country open to total submission to the English enemy.

Dunbar Castle, East Lothian. Here, in the castle they had hoped to relieve, many of the Scottish knights, run off the battlefield on 27 April 1297, ignominiously sought shelter (Historic Scotland).

CHAPTER 3

'FOR SO LONG AS ONE HUNDRED OF US REMAIN ALIVE...'

THE WARS OF INDEPENDENCE TO THE MID 14TH CENTURY

OPPOSITE: *William Wallace. The importance of Wallace is that he demonstrated to his countrymen that it was possible to mount an effective resistance to the English and defeat them (Ian Shepherd).*

After the rout of the Scottish army at Dunbar in April 1296 Edward I of England progressed round Scotland, securing the country and the submission of the nobles and landholders. King John was ignominiously stripped of his kingship and led off to England. An English administration was imposed and garrisons installed. But this apparent consolidation of England's hold on Scotland was only to be the opening phase in a long struggle which was to see the ultimate victory of the Scots.

WILLIAM WALLACE THE GUARDIAN

After 1296 opposition to the English was carried on by a series of guardians in the name of the deposed King John. The guardians included leading Scots of the day, Robert Bruce, John Comyn, John de Soules, the bishops of St Andrews and Glasgow, often in uneasy coalition. The first of the guardians, William Wallace, was the most remarkable, and of the greatest importance in helping the Scottish recovery and influencing the Scots' self image.

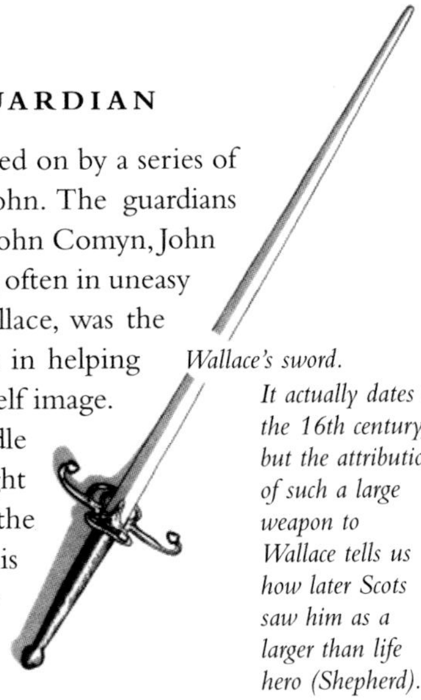

Unlike all other Scottish leaders of the Middle Ages, Wallace was not a great lord, nor even a knight when he rose to prominence, but merely the younger son of a Lowland laird. The details of his life are obscure. Whether he was thrust forward by noble patrons, James the Stewart and Bishop Wishart of Glasgow, or whether he was merely

Wallace's sword. It actually dates to the 16th century, but the attribution of such a large weapon to Wallace tells us how later Scots saw him as a larger than life hero (Shepherd).

31

an outlaw who hit the big time, is unimportant. What matters is that he was a man unswerving in his attachment to the national cause and was able to threaten the English hold on Scotland at a time when others dared not.

STIRLING BRIDGE AND FALKIRK

By the summer of 1297 Wallace was joint leader with Andrew Murray of a considerable army. Murray belonged to one of the great noble families in Scotland with lands in the north-east. How much of the credit for the battle of Stirling Bridge rightly belongs to him rather than Wallace is not known for he died soon afterwards, possibly from wounds. On their route to Stirling, Wallace and Murray had besieged and captured castles, but more than that, along with other unsung heroes, they had all but dismantled the machinery of English government. Such officials who were still in place were confined to their castles, and it was impossible to administer the surrounding countryside or collect taxes.

View of the Wallace Monument, showing the site of the Battle of Stirling Bridge (Caldwell).

On 11 September the Scottish army was positioned on the Abbey Craig to the north of the River Forth, watching the bridge to Stirling. The English army of retribution, commanded by the Earl of Surrey and Hugh Cressingham, respectively English Lieutenant and Treasurer of Scotland, were on the south bank of the river. The Battle of Dunbar and other dealings with the Scots had taught them to have absolutely no respect for their opponents, and they saw no problem about getting to their prey as quickly as possible by leading their army across the narrow bridge - a slow business. The sizes of the two armies are not reliably known but the English was undoubtedly the larger and better equipped. It also had a considerable force of cavalry while the Scots were all on foot.

In hindsight it is easy to see what Wallace and Murray had to do – and do it they did, coolly and precisely. They waited only for as much of the English army as they reckoned they could confidently handle to cross the bridge, and then descended upon it. The winding of the river and soft ground meant the English were caught in a trap, unable to deploy their horse successfully, or get back across the bridge for the press of traffic, as more of the army attempted to come forward. The result was an overwhelming victory for the Scots. The English on the north side of the river were slaughtered, including Cressingham, and the rest on the south side were led off to Berwick in haste by Surrey.

The Scots were soon in effective control of all of Scotland but for a few castles, and in October and November Wallace was able to mount a devastating raid into England, looting and burning as far as Cockermouth on the west and to the River Tyne in the east. It could not be expected that Edward I would leave matters there, and in the summer of 1298 he duly put together a formidable army and set out to find Wallace. His army had some 2,000 cavalry and 12,000 foot, and was opposed at Falkirk by the Scots, hardly more than 8,000 strong, and possibly a lot less.

Wallace had drawn his army out on a piece of rising ground, fronted by a boggy area. The bulk of his force were footmen armed with spears and these were placed in four circular formations, each protected all round with wooden stakes roped together. With spears thrusting out in all directions these schiltroms, as they were called in contemporary accounts, had the appearance of enormous hedgehogs. Archers from the Forest of Selkirk were placed in the spaces between the schiltroms and a small force of cavalry was drawn up behind.

Although the schiltroms withstood the attacks of the English cavalry for some time, they got little support from their own horse and archers, the former having precipitately fled, and the archers having been mowed down. This left the field free for King Edward to bring up his archers and crossbowmen to rain missiles into the Scottish foot. It was only a matter of time before there were not enough men in the schiltroms to fill the gaps and the English cavalry could ride in and wreak a terrible slaughter.

The defeat at Falkirk was a devastating blow to the cause of Scottish resistance. Wallace was discredited as a national leader, and the guardians who succeeded him avoided major confrontations with the enemy. To step up the pressure, the English campaigned in Scotland throughout the winter of 1301-1302. By 1305 Edward I was effectively back in control of Scotland and all the leading Scots had submitted to him. William Wallace had been captured and executed in London – with the most savage butchery – for rebelling against a king he had never recognised.

SCOTTISH STRENGTHS AND WEAKNESSES

The year 1305 did not, of course, mark the end of the struggle but it is a good point to pause and consider what had gone wrong for the Scots. Yes, they had had some remarkable successes, particularly at Stirling Bridge, and had shown remarkable resilience and persistence when faced with the sustained push of the great English war machine.

Yeomen following their king into battle (Mark Dennis).

On the other hand, Dunbar in 1296 had demonstrated that the Scots could not field an adequate force of heavy horse, the only element in an army of that time deemed of any real worth in battle. Despite a small victory at Roslin in 1303 by the Scottish horse it was a very long time before it was again to be viewed as the elite unit, the winning stroke in battle.

The bulk of Wallace's army at Stirling Bridge and Falkirk, the spearmen who fought on foot, were not of noble blood, or knights or holders of large tracts of land. They were the yeomanry, the more substantial folk who worked the land themselves. Their commitment to fight may have depended on their requirement to do service in the host but it is remarkable that the Scottish guardians in the years up to 1305 were often able to keep them in the field for months at a time, not just on lucrative raids into England but campaigning in Scotland in attempts to contain or harry English forces. To anticipate, it was these yeomen, not Robert Bruce's famous band of noble captains, who were given the credit of defeating the English by an experienced leader on the English side, a Scotsman himself. In Barbour's poem, the Bruce, Sir Ingram Umfraville (*c.*1323) advises the English king to make a long truce with the Scots in the hope that the Scottish yeomen,

OPPOSITE: *A 14th-century tomb slab at Iona with the effigy of Gille-Brigde MacKinnon, who is said to have fought for Bruce at Bannockburn. He has the sword, spear, gloves of plate, aketon and basinet, required by the legislation of 1318 (Shepherd).*

who through long experience of warfare are as good as knights, will return to their farming and lose their military skills.

By 1323 there must indeed have been many experienced yeomen in Scottish armies. The credit for demonstrating that they were a force to be reckoned with should go to Wallace. Even though Falkirk was a major defeat it was not because his men did not stand long, resolutely fighting against the odds. The fact that they are all said to have been armed with spears contrasts with descriptions of earlier Scottish armies where axes were much more in evidence. It is possible that Wallace was responsible for this total adoption of the spear as a deliberate tactic for countering cavalry. It is known that the English lost over 100 horses, perhaps over 200, at Falkirk, presumably speared by the Scottish foot.

There were many in Europe aware of the fighting in Scotland and the major engagements. It is a moot point whether the leaders of the Flemish spearmen who defeated the mounted knights of France at Courtrai in 1302 were aware of Wallace and his battles. Robert Bruce, very probably at Falkirk, would almost certainly have known about Courtrai and could have drawn conclusions as to why the Flemings were so successful while the Scots had failed.

We have no clues as to whether Wallace seriously contemplated not fighting the English in 1297 and 1298, but withdrawing before them. His success at Stirling Bridge had demonstrated the enormous gains in morale and territory that were consequent on a victory on the battlefield. Although the English never effectively controlled all the countryside of Scotland, their hold on towns and castles, many of which could be supplied from the sea, was like a cancer, waiting to burst forth again whenever the Scots stumbled. Opinions are divided as to whether the Scots could ultimately have achieved their independence without squaring up to the English in battle, but they certainly had to find the medicine for dealing with the English strongholds in their realm.

THE REQUIRED DRESS

The Parliament held by Robert Bruce at Scone in 1318 enacted the minimum levels of military equipment required for the different classes of fighting men. Men worth £10 in goods were to have a sword, spear and gloves of plate and an aketon and a basinet, or a habergeon and an iron hat; those having goods to the value of a cow were to be armed with a spear or a bow. Aketons were quilted coats worn either by themselves or under armour for added defence; basinets were simple conical helmets which became more popular than the heavy helmets which completely enveloped the head. Habergeons were mail coats, lighter than the hauberks worn earlier. There is no mention of horses; these were now essentially for transport, for limited use on the battlefield or for chasing the fleeing enemy afterwards.

BRUCE'S TESTAMENT

Although Bruce himself fought pitched battles he is said to have enjoined his successors to employ the following simple and effective strategy in warfare: firstly, they should never enter into a pitched battle with the English but harry them with light skirmishing; secondly, they should never fortify their towns with walls but defend them by force of arms. The odds were certainly normally against the Scots when it came to set battles, and even if they won, it was likely that the English could make a quick recovery and field another army. If defeated, there was little chance of raising another force and they lost not only men but often valuable equipment. Many Scottish towns did eventually have walls around them, but mostly of no strength to withstand a determined enemy.

A portrait of Robert Bruce? This picture is based on a detailed examination of the king's skull, using computer technology to reconstruct the muscles and skin. It was made by staff of the University of Edinburgh's Centre for Dental Education and the Edinburgh Dental Hospital (by kind permission of Dr R I MacLeod).

ROBERT THE BRUCE

If Edward I in 1306 had thought he had finally cracked Scottish resistance he was soon to receive a rude shock when the Earl of Carrick, Robert Bruce, not only raised a new rebellion but had himself crowned king at Scone. Any hope that John Balliol could ever be reinstated as king had by now disappeared and Bruce did, in fact, have a very good case to be considered as rightful heir, but this action – not to mention the murder in church of his main rival, John Comyn – inevitably offended many Scots. His uprising was all but finished in the first two years, with Bruce and a small band of followers hunted fugitives, and to win through he not only had to deal with the English but many powerful Scots as well.

Bruce was ultimately successful in freeing Scotland from the English and having his own right to be king recognised. He was a great statesman, but above all, the greatest military leader in the history of Scotland.

Bruce developed successful ways of capturing enemy strongholds. The Scots did on occasion use siege engines, and had access to military engineers, but in the years leading up to Bannockburn there appeared few castles or towns that could not fall to a night attack using a very simple piece of equipment – a ladder. Even the rock of

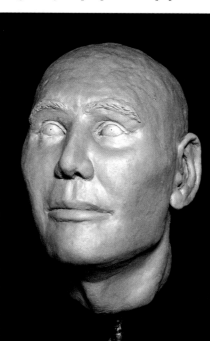

Edinburgh Castle was climbed and the walls scaled in 1314 while a diversion was created at the main entrance. Bruce had a devastatingly simple solution to such castles being reoccupied and held against him – he destroyed them, and filled in their wells.

There is a fairly general assumption that Bruce did not believe in fighting battles and that somehow his greatest victory – at Bannockburn in 1314 – was a mistake. His brother Edward had made an agreement in

1313 with the commander of Stirling Castle, then one of the last major strongholds in English hands, that unless he was relieved in a year he would hand the castle over. But Bruce's biographer, Barbour, has him rebuke his brother, not for making the truce, but for making it so long that the English king would have plenty of time to gather a large army. Bruce readily assumes the English king will offer battle to stop the castle being taken. In fact, Bruce willingly fights on several occasions. In the Pass of Brander in Argyll in 1308 he readily sees how he can circumvent a poorly prepared ambush and turn the tables on his Macdougall foes. At Byland in Yorkshire in 1322 he launches a frontal attack up a hill on a considerable force under the Duke of Richmond. Such boldness in attack is, however, uncharacteristic, and at both the Pass of Brander and Byland the day was won thanks to flank attacks swinging the balance in Bruce's favour at the critical moment. Bruce won such battles because he could see how to do so with limited losses on his own side, and because he had the confidence and timing to succeed.

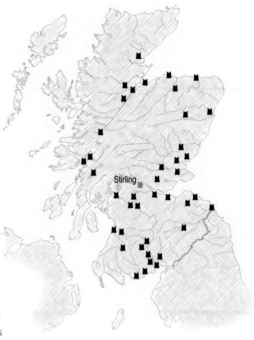

Castles held by, or for, the English in the early 14th century. By 1314 Stirling was the only important one left in central Scotland (after G W S Barrow).

Bruce was personally hardy, and when appropriate, brave to the extent of foolhardiness. When he captured Perth in 1313 Bruce led the way in the dark through the moat and was the second man over the town wall. More significantly, in the run up to the Battle of Bannockburn, in full view of his men, Bruce stood his ground when an English knight launched a surprise attack upon him. Although only riding a pony, he side-stepped the Englishman's lance and broke his axe in a blow

The siege of Carlisle in 1315, from an English charter of 1316. It depicts on the left the Scots using a stone-throwing machine. More typical is the attempt, shown on the right, to scale the walls by ladder (after 1316 charter in Carlisle Record Office).

Robert Bruce riding into battle: the statue beside the site of Bannockburn (Caldwell).

which sliced right through his opponent's helmet and head. What better way to inspire his men before the most crucial battle in Scottish history?

Perhaps more typical of the man and his strategy is his calculated caution. This is especially evident in the devastating raids mounted into the north of England, as far as Yorkshire, either led by himself, or his trusted captains, especially Thomas Randolph and James Douglas. The aim was normally to avoid battle and plunder where they would not or could not collect blackmail; but their boldness was always balanced by careful intelligence work and timing. Bruce's caution, but determination to fight is seen in two battles where he consciously demonstrates the lessons to be learned from Falkirk and probably Courtrai, adopting defensive tactics.

The first was in 1307 when his force was only a few hundred strong and he had no successes behind him to inspire his followers or draw more to his cause. He was being pursued by a large force of English horse commanded by Aymer de Valence, who had defeated Bruce at Methven the year before. Barbour claims that de Valence challenged Bruce to stay and fight him below Loudoun Hill in Ayrshire on 10 May. Be that as it may, Bruce did wait for de Valence, but made careful preparations. He chose a level field flanked on both sides by bogs. His men fought all on foot but were not to be imprisoned in a corral of roped stakes. Instead Bruce had ditches dug well in front of his men, designed to impede - not stop - the English attack, and bunch their horses together. As at Courtrai, this took the sting out of the cavalry charge, to which de Valence had committed half his force. Bruce had given his men enough room to manouevre so that they were able to move forward, pushing the defeated English vanguard back into the ditches, or in confusion on to their own rearguard. Soon the whole enemy force was in precipitate flight and the news of Bruce's success had a dramatic effect in increasing his stature and following amongst his own people. Loudoun Hill demonstrated that the Scottish spearmen were not only steady enough to stand up to an English cavalry charge but could defeat it.

Extent of Scottish raiding into England under Bruce

1318 (recapture of Berwick)

1317

1317

Newcastle

Carlisle

Extent of Scottish raiding

Durham

1322

1322   1319

York

Battles (with dates) won by Scots

BANNOCKBURN

At Bannockburn Bruce used similar tactics against the full might of King Edward II. He chose his position well, and by denying them enough firm ground to manoeuvre on, prevented the full development of the much-feared English cavalry attack. His men were drawn up in four battles, perhaps only a total of 5-6000, including small contingents of archers and horse, facing an army three times that size, well-equipped, and with a strike force of over 2000 cavalry.

As so often before, it was the English cavalry which was first committed to battle, but in long and desperate fighting it failed to break the Scottish foot units. Whereas at Falkirk the English archers and crossbowmen had decimated the Scottish ranks, now at Bannockburn Bruce kept his small force of horse specifically to chase the English archers away before they could do such damage. Bruce committed all four of his schiltroms to battle, pushing forward against an increasingly demoralised and packed English army, hemmed in by boggy ground and water courses. It is said that the last straw for many of the English was the appearance of a body of Scottish servants and labourers ('small folk'), anxious to take part in the fighting. They were

Battle of Bannockburn: 3 phases of fighting on 24 June 1314

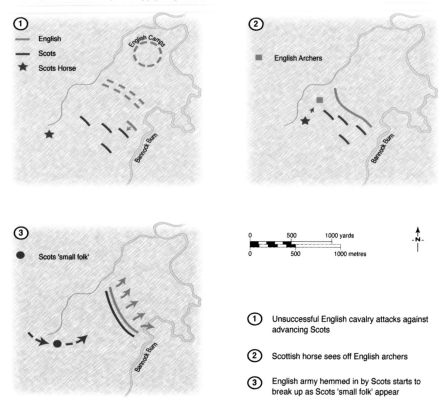

① Unsuccessful English cavalry attacks against advancing Scots

② Scottish horse sees off English archers

③ English army hemmed in by Scots starts to break up as Scots 'small folk' appear

mistaken for a fresh Scottish army. Soon all that could were in headlong flight, many thousands killed at the hands of the Scots, trampled underfoot, or drowned in the water. Edward II, personally a brave and experienced soldier, only just got safely away.

Decisive though Bannockburn was it was not enough to end the war once and for all. For that Bruce had to patiently demonstrate to his foes over many years that it was not worthwhile meddling with Scotland. He took the war into England, raiding and collecting blackmail as far as Yorkshire. By 1327 he was even set on annexing Northumberland. He attacked English interests in Ireland, his brother Edward being crowned king of that country in 1316, and he was able to control western seaways, raiding as far as Angelsey and the Isle of Man. Nevertheless it was not until 1327, almost at the end of Bruce's life, that the English finally recognised him as king and the independence of his country.

It would be a source of great satisfaction for all Scots if Bruce's

OPPOSITE TOP: *The Battle of Bannockburn after the early 15th-century Scottish manuscript, the Scotichronicon. Drawn a century after the battle, it depicts the scene using arms and armour current at that time (Shepherd).*

achievements had neatly brought to an end the struggle with England, but that was not to be. The governors who ruled Scotland on behalf of the young David II after Bruce's death in 1329 had to contend with invasions by those supporters of the English cause who had been dispossessed by Bruce, attempts to have King John's son, Edward Balliol, installed as king, and further attempts at annexation by the new English king, Edward III. The Scots made many mistakes, but they had learned they could ...intain their independence and they had the resolve to do so. These Wars of Independence left the Scots with an enduring distrust of their neighbours, a dogged determination to win through against the odds, and a belief in their own military prowess, even if it was sometimes inflated. This is aptly expressed in the 1320 Declaration of Arbroath, a letter in the name of the leading Scots to the Pope, a potent declaration of independence:

'For so long as one hundred of us remain alive, we will never consent to subject ourselves to the dominion of the English. For it is not glory, it is not riches, neither is it honour, but it is liberty alone that we fight and contend for, which no honest man will lose but with his life.'

By the 1340s Edward III had decided there was no honour and glory for him in Scotland and turned to richer pickings in France.

LESSONS LEARNED

The Wars of Independence were a painful learning experience for the Scots. There would have been few who would have felt flattered by the adoption and adaptation of some of their successful tactics by their enemies, although the English did, in fact, do so. The English army which fought and defeated the rebel force under Thomas of Lancaster at Boroughbridge in 1322 was composed of northern levies of foot, drawn up in schiltroms like the Scots. The failure of their men of arms at Bannockburn led them to dismount for battle, even when, as with the fighting in France, they had to face mounted charges from the French. The devastating raids by mounted Scottish forces deep into England are believed to be the model for English campaigns in France during the Hundred Years' War (1338-1453).

The statue of Robert Bruce at Stirling Castle (Caldwell).

CHAPTER 4

CHIVALRY VERSUS GUNS

WARFARE OF THE MID 14TH TO MID 15TH CENTURIES

Throughout the Middle Ages the Scots were adept at raiding into England and minimising the damage in their own country from English counter-measures. For these hit and run tactics horses were used for speed, and armour and equipment was light.

The Scots preferred simple iron hats - kettle hats or sallets - aketons, or jackets reinforced with metal plates - jacks or brigandines. They fought on foot with axes, spears, swords and bows and arrows.

RAID AND COUNTER-RAID

The events of 1385 show this sort of fighting in classic form. In that year the French sent an expeditionary force of 1000 men of arms and 500 crossbowmen under the command of the French Admiral, Jean de Vienne. He also brought money and armour to encourage the Scots to invade England. It was intended that this should coincide with a direct landing of French troops further south in England but this never materialised. The Scottish host was called out and together with the French an invasion in strength was made into the East March (the eastern border country), capturing and destroying the important frontier castle of Wark and two lesser strongholds, Cornhill and Ford. The country was burnt as far as Morpeth when word came of an approaching English army under the Duke of Lancaster. Much to the disgust of the French the Scots refused to stay and fight but led off their booty and prepared to lay waste their own country to leave nothing for their enemy to get their hands on.

Lancaster's force was merely the advanced guard of an even larger army under the banner of the young king Richard II, an army which, if not as sizeable as the 60,000 or so ascribed to it by an early chronicler, was certainly very large. From the mid-14th century on it was normal English practice that armies for

OPPOSITE: *Mons Meg, made in Mons in 1449, given to James II by the Duke of Burgundy in 1457. The carriage is a modern reproduction of one made for sea service in 1540 (Historic Scotland).*

Carving of a man with a fighting axe on a 15th-century tomb front at Coupar Angus Church (Shepherd).

The Scots and French capture Wark Castle in 1385. After a rather fanciful contemporary illustration from Froissart's Chronicle (Shepherd).

war against the Scots were raised only from the counties to the north of the Trent but on this occasion, to do honour to the young king and out of fear of the French intervention, contingents were drawn from further south as well. The abbeys of Dryburgh, Melrose and Newbattle were destroyed and Edinburgh occupied and burnt but the English did not penetrate any further into the country. Although the raid was pursued with the utmost severity the Scots' policy in deserting and laying waste their own countryside was paying off. The English found little of value to pillage and, more serious for them, no food, this probably being the main reason why they had to withdraw after a few days.

Meanwhile the leaders of the Scottish and French forces, having seen that the English army was too large for them to tackle, launched a new and devastating raid into the English West March (the western borders). They returned home to a country coming alive again with the folk returning with their animals from the woods and hills, ready to re-erect their flimsy dwellings once more. While we might question the need for the raids of 1385 and have reservations about whether the destruction wrought by the Scots and the booty gained was worth the burning of Edinburgh and the abbeys, it is clear from a military point of view that the Scots were

The abbey of Melrose in the Border country, one of those destroyed in English raiding for the young king, Richard II (Caldwell).

successful. They could get more that was of value to them out of pillaging in England than the English could get from Scotland. More than that, it cost the Scottish government nothing to put an army into the field, but a great deal of money in wages and expenses for the English to do likewise, and it was certainly not good for morale or the prestige of the king to fail to find an enemy to defeat in battle.

A major factor in the Scots' success in 1385 was good intelligence, knowing well in advance when the enemy was on the move, and maintaining sufficient contact at all times to predict which way they would turn. It was lack of good intelligence that turned other raids into disasters, most spectacularly in 1346 when the young King David II was forced to fight at Neville's Cross near Durham and was taken prisoner, and in 1402 when a Scottish army 10,000 strong, led by Archibald 'The Tyneman' (ie the loser), fourth Earl of Douglas, was caught at Homildonhill near Wooler and taken apart by a devastating display of English archery.

The Scots' hit and run tactics were all very well when they were successful, but even so many looked to do things differently. The acquisition of honour and glory was of considerable importance and these were not necessarily to be accrued from destruction and plunder and the avoidance of battles. Warfare in the Middle Ages, just as now, was often thought of in terms of battles. It was dishonourable and cowardly to avoid them. Only on a battlefield could a general's true skill be seen, and Scotland did not lack aspiring generals although she was, unfortunately, not blessed with many of any ability.

HIGHLAND WARFARE

By the late 14th century it was clear to the Scots that their country contained two nations distinguishable by their different languages, manners and customs. Many of the Gaelic speakers belonged to the powerful Lordship of the Isles in the west. The powerful MacDonald lords could field armies several thousand strong, and far-ranging fleets. They clashed several times with the Stewart kings before James IV finally stripped them of their lands and titles in 1493.

Representations of West Highland gentry on their grave slabs indicate that, down to the 16th century, they continued to wear basinets and aketons, light and flexible gear suitable for their mountainous terrain and guerrilla warfare. Many men from the West Highlands also went to fight as mercenaries in Ireland, many settling down there as a more or less permanent military caste.

A grave slab at Finlaggan, Islay, with the effigy of Donald MacGillespie, mid 16th century. He wears a basinet and an aketon with mail over his shoulders (Caldwell).

OTTERBURN – A TRIUMPH FOR CHIVALRY

In 1388 a Scottish force won a famous victory at Otterburn, which it probably had no need to fight, and in so doing both the leading Scots and the English they vanquished stepped into the pages of history and romance as the epitome of all that was noble and honourable in medieval warfare. The battle itself with its hand to hand fighting was a fit place for heroes. Here the skies were not darkened by a forest of arrows or the explosion of guns which downed brave and coward alike before their prowess could be put to the test.

The Scots capture Percy's pennon and display it in their camp outside Newcastle; after a manuscript in the Biblioteka Narodowa, Warsaw (Shepherd).

The Scottish force numbered no more than about 200 men of arms and 2,000 'foot', all mounted, and was led by James, Second Earl of Douglas and the two Dunbar brothers, the Earls of Moray and March. It was engaged on a raid down to Durham as a diversion for a larger invasion in the west, led by the Earl of Fife and Sir Archibald Douglas. So successful was the smaller Scottish force that by the time it was returning northwards the English warden, Henry Percy ('Hotspur'), had still not mustered all his troops but was caught within Newcastle by the Scots who, for show more than any serious intent to capture the town, encamped outside. Here some skirmishing took place and the Earl of Douglas captured Percy's pennon.

Douglas is said to have boasted that he would plant it outside his tent that night to see if Percy would dare to come and recover it. Percy did not, but the Scots, aware that the English forces were gathering, prudently withdrew early the next day, heading north-west for Jedburgh. On the way, they captured and destroyed a tower house at Ponteland and camped the night at Otterburn. The next two days were spent unsuccessfully besieging the towerhouse at Otterburn, by which time Percy had discovered that Douglas' army was not, as he had first suspected, the vanguard of the main invasion in the West but a separate force, and with an army of about 8000 foot and 600 horse set off in pursuit to get his revenge.

The English reached Otterburn on the evening of the Scots' second day there and, although it was already getting dark, Percy pressed on to catch his enemy unawares in their camp. The accounts of the actual conflict are as confused as the fighting must have been. Much of it seems to have been done by the light of the moon so that it was too dark for the English to use their bows to good effect.

Arrowheads, rusted together, from Urquhart Castle, Loch Ness. Scottish Governments encouraged the use of bows and arrows for warfare (National Museums of Scotland).

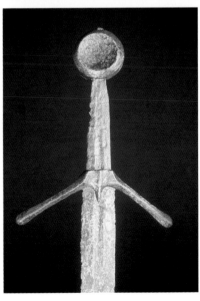

Instead both sides got to grips with each other with spears, axes, swords and daggers. Also, because of the confused nature of the battle, much of the fighting developed into man to man struggles in true heroic fashion. Sometime in the course of the night the Douglas himself was felled, by whom is not known. The chronicler Jean Froissart, who had seen Douglas as a boy and who talked to knights who fought in the battle, even managed to record appropriate dying words – that he thanked God that like most of his ancestors he died thus and not in his bed.

Despite the death of Douglas there was no doubting that the victory was the Scots'. No other Scots of importance are recorded as being killed, but the English suffered heavily, and all their top men, including Hotspur and his brother Ralph Percy, were captured. Otterburn confirmed the fighting ability of the Scots and considerably enhanced their reputation on

Scottish sword of c. 1400. Swords were expensive, the blades imported from the Continent, and were used by the nobles and gentry (National Museums of Scotland).

TOURNAMENTS

Tournaments offered young noble warriors opportunities for training and renown. King David II indulged his interest in them while a prisoner in London in the 1340s and 1350s. The fame of the Douglas family attracted the attention of the Burgundian knight, Jacques de Lalain, the epitome of chivalry who wandered Europe looking for worthy opponents. In 1448 Lalain and two companions fought two of the Douglases and the Laird of Halket at Stirling before James II, the three foreigners evidently having the best of the contest. Chivalry was to have a last fling in Scotland in the early 16th century with the tournaments staged in Edinburgh by James IV. (Illustration by Mark Dennis).

the Continent. Their skill in dealing with an enemy who they could get to grips with in hand to hand fighting was again shown notably in 1419 at Baugé in France when a Scottish expeditionary force under the Earls of Buchan and Wigton bore the brunt of the fighting against an attacking English army, killing its commander the Duke of Clarence, and capturing other leaders.

Warfare as practised in the medieval period was a grim disgusting business but chivalric sentiments could create for it a veneer of respectability or even a set of ideals to which some aspired and a few sought to attain. The Scots were caught up in the chivalric notions of the day and their flirtation with them by no means began or ended with Otterburn. Perhaps the clearest indication of the spirit of chivalry that affected the country is the series of jousts or single-combats arranged between nobles on both sides of the Border. The most famous was that held on London Bridge (illustrated below) in 1390 between Sir David Lindsay of Glenesk and John Lord Welles, in which the Englishman was unhorsed.

In 1403 even the governor, Albany, was prepared to put the whole kingdom in jeopardy by raising the fencibles to relieve the unimportant castle of Cocklaw in Roxburghshire because its keeper had promised Henry Percy that he would surrender it unless rescued by the King of Scots or the governor in six weeks. As it happened the English failed to meet Albany's challenge, possibly because the whole incident was stage-managed by Percy to give him an excuse to raise an army against his own king, Henry IV.

GUNS AND CASTLES

Even as chivalry blossomed among the Scots as a military ethic, they adopted something which was to be much more important in warfare in the longer term - guns. Contemporary documents indicate that the Scots were using guns, small pieces of artillery, by the 1380s. The siege of Roxburgh Castle by James I in 1436 may have been the first occasion on which the Scots tried to exploit their potential to knock down walls. Although this siege was unsuccessful, artillery trains were used to good effect by James II in the 1450s, in particular at Abercorn Castle, a house of the Black Douglases, which fell in 1455. James himself wrote to Charles VII of France telling how he besieged the castle for a month and, having knocked down the towers on its curtain walls with non-stop fire from his guns, stormed and took it.

Close-up of a gun-loop of c.1460 at Ravenscraig Castle, Fife (Caldwell).

Some guns were made in Scotland, others were got from abroad like the massive gun James acquired in 1457 as a gift from his uncle, Duke Philip the Good of Burgundy. This gun, known then as Mons (later Mons Meg)(chapter frontispiece), is probably the largest gun ever seen in Scotland. She was commissioned by the duke from Jehan Cambier of Mons and was completed in 1449. She fired 18 inch (457mm) stone balls and was still being used on active service a century later. Not all early guns were so effective as Mons. Like her, they were normally made of wrought iron, but many were loaded by wedging a separate chamber with the powder and shot at the breech end. While this meant that guns could achieve a good rate of fire by the simple expedient of having more than one chamber for each, an obvious disadvantage was the design weakness of having a join in the

The castle on an island in Lochleven, an early example of a tower-house, possibly dating to the early 14th century (Historic Scotland).

The curtain wall, Threave Castle, mid 15th century, well provided with gun-loops and towers for flanking fire (Historic Scotland).

barrel just where the powder exploded. James II achieved the unenviable distinction of being the first ruler to die by means of a gun when one of his own blew up at the siege of Roxburgh Castle in 1460.

The Wars of Independence had taught the Scottish nobility the folly of investing too heavily in castles as a protection against an enemy. The dominant architectural form of the 14th to the 16th century is the tower-house. They were conceived primarily as family residences and it is evident that any military role was secondary. Indeed most were built by lesser members of the nobility who could not maintain large households or bodies of retainers. Typically they had storage space at ground floor, the main hall at first floor level, and private accommodation in one or more stories above. Thick walls, small windows and stoutly secured doors gave them strength against attack, but there is often nothing more than a walkway protected by a parapet round the wall-top from which to pursue an active defence. They were normally but one element in a residential grouping including other domestic or farmyard structures.

A reconstruction of the siege of Threave in 1455 (Historic Scotland).

The advent of guns put all Scottish castles at risk and by the mid 15th century there is some evidence of thought being given to how to use, or counter, the new technology. The curtain wall at the Douglas castle at Threave in Galloway has loops for small guns and projecting round towers at the corners from which flanking fire could be provided. What is more, the walls have an external batter to give strength and deflect enemy shot. These defences are thought to have been in place by the time the castle was besieged and taken by James II in 1455. At Ravenscraig Castle on a sea-girt promontory in Fife, built for James II's queen, Mary of Gueldres about 1460, there are also gunloops, but here the intention of the builder appears to have been to hide the main bulk of the massive landward walls behind the counterscarp of a ditch where besieging guns could not reach.

The landward defences of Ravenscraig Castle, c. 1460, protected by a deep ditch from enemy bombardment (Caldwell).

CHAPTER 5

ASSAULT AND BATTERY

TAKING GUNS AGAINST THE ENGLISH, 1496-1523

OPPOSITE: Edinburgh Castle. James IV established a gun foundry here at the beginning of the 16th century. There were also storehouses and workshops for the repair and manufacture of weapons and military equipment (Historic Scotland).

In **the second half** of the 15th century guns were greatly improved in many ways, especially in the Low Countries and France, and up-to-date artillery soon appeared in Scotland. The Scots eagerly adopted this new technology and used it as the principle element in an aggressive foreign policy directed against England.

The new guns were of cast bronze, which was much stronger, and fired metal shot which packed a bigger punch than the stone shot fired from wrought-iron guns. They had trunnions on both sides of the barrel for ease in mounting on carriages which could be pulled over rough country much more readily than the older gun carts.

GUNS AND PIKES

James III is said to have had a train of French artillery and was responsible for first casting bronze guns in Edinburgh (by 1474), but it was not until the establishment of a foundry in Edinburgh Castle in 1511 that we have clear evidence that guns were being successfully manufactured, at first with French personnel under the direction of Robert Borthwick. This foundry remained in operation until 1558 but only ever produced a small proportion of the artillery and equipment needed by the Scots. Most had to be imported from the Continent, normally at great expense.

The other significant development in military affairs was the wholesale adoption by the Scots of the pike and all that that entailed in methods of fighting. Pikes were essentially very long spears. As early as 1471, an Act of Parliament forbade merchants from importing – or Scottish bowyers from making – spears of less than six ells in length (over 5.5m or 18ft). Swiss and German mercenaries had demonstrated how effective pikes could be when put in the hands of well trained and drilled battalions of men. Their great length meant that several ranks could be presented to an enemy in serried rows,

A small bronze field gun cast in Edinburgh Castle. It has the royal arms and initials of James V (1513-42). It was found in Loch Semple, Renfrewshire, and may have been lost at the siege of the castle there in 1560 (by kind permission of Glasgow Museum and Art Galleries).

King James III as he would have appeared at the Battle of Sauchieburn in 1488, with plate armour from head to toe. He was murdered in the confusion surrounding his defeat and flight. Gold quarter rider of James III (National Museums of Scotland).

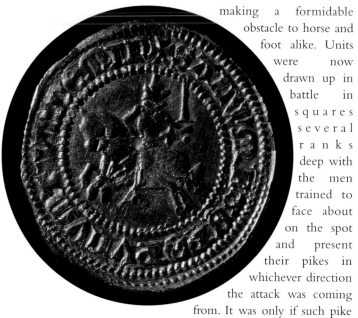

making a formidable obstacle to horse and foot alike. Units were now drawn up in battle in squares several ranks deep with the men trained to face about on the spot and present their pikes in whichever direction the attack was coming from. It was only if such pike units became disarranged or dispersed that they could be defeated, because then the length of the pikes became a severe encumbrance to their owners.

In the Battle of Sauchieburn in 1488 both sides were drawn up in the traditional way into a vanguard, main battle and rearguard, many on horse, and armed with a range of weapons. The Scottish army at Flodden in 1513 fought in four pike units.

A PROMISING BEGINNING IN 1496

James IV's first expedition into England was in 1496 and it set the pattern for warfare with that country for the rest of his reign and the succeeding governorship of Albany. It may be described as an attempt to win an advantage over the English by open assault and battery of their frontier fortifications. Attention was concentrated on the East Marches and it is likely that a longer term objective was the isolation and recovery of Berwick, last in Scottish hands in 1482. The town itself was considered too strong to succumb to assault straight away, though the English were in constant fear of the Scots attempting this. With a large army to scare off relief from neighbouring strongholds the Scots could hope to concentrate on reducing a major fortress with their guns, a fairly predictable exercise given enough time.

Ranks of pikemen were a major development in the Scottish military approach (Historic Scotland).

Time, in fact, was one of the most crucial elements in this strategy. It took a good week for the guns to be hauled over the

James IV's raid into England, September 1496

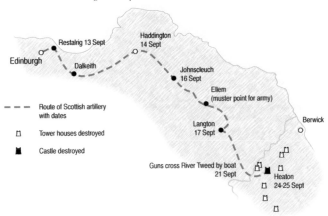

The raid of 1496 was a success. The Scots did much damage and got away safely. But note how it took over a week to get the guns to the border, and four days later they had to return as an English army advanced from Newcastle

Lammermuirs from Edinburgh to the River Tweed and in both 1496 and 1497 James adopted the expensive expedient of hiring horses which were faster and more efficient than levies of plough-oxen. Even so the guns had to be accompanied by numerous wrights, smiths and labourers armed with shovels, spades and picks 'to draw the gunnis in peththis and myris'. The money to pay for all the necessary equipment and hire of men and horses was in short supply and the host could only be kept together for a short time. No doubt it was considered prudent in any case not to remain on the offensive too long but leave time in hand to counter English retaliatory invasions. In 1496 the Scots remained in the field for a fortnight or less and in 1497 for only a few days longer.

Another important consideration was the speed with which the English, well served with reports from spies, could send an army to the Border, for it was not a

Norham Castle on the Tweed, an important English Border fortress, bombarded unsuccessfully in 1497, and taken in 1513 (Richard Oram).

NAVAL WARFARE

Both James III and James IV were interested in ships and their potential in warfare. In 1489 Sir Alexander Wood, with two ships, defeated an English fleet of five off Dunbar. The following year Wood again triumphed over three English ships seeking revenge. After a two-day struggle involving guns, pots of lime and fireballs, followed by hand-to-hand fighting, the English were taken captive to Dundee. James IV used his ships to campaign in the west against the Lords of the Isles, and in 1502 sent a fleet to the Baltic to aid the Danes against the Swedes. He built a dockyard at Newhaven for constructing large ships, and a more secure dry dock further up the Forth at Airth for fitting out and repair.

part of Scottish strategy to wait and fight. Thus, between getting the guns to the Border and the arrival of an English army, there were only a very few days available in which the Scots could prosecute a siege and withdraw safely. In 1496 James had time to use his guns for four or five days at the most. In the following year Norham Castle survived being battered by Mons Meg for no more than four days though it fell in six in 1513. In 1523 it was the turn of Wark Castle: it survived the two day bombardment Albany meted out to it though it is doubtful if it could have survived a third.

It was probably no accident that the Scots preferred to campaign late in the season. Not only might they hope to do more damage to the ripe or harvested corn, but by the end of the campaign their own crops would be safely harvested and the weather, with luck, would have broken down, making any immediate retaliation by the English more difficult. Certainly in 1497, 1513 and again in 1523 the bad weather was a major contributory factor in saving Scotland from the full force of English vengeance.

James' raid of 1496 may be said to have been a success. The important fortress of the Grays at Heaton succumbed to his guns, aided by his quarriers who dug a mine to destroy its walls. The castle was left as a ruin which was never repaired. Meanwhile his army had spread out and laid waste the English East Marches a distance of seven miles into the countryside, destroying eight tower-houses. All managed to withdraw safely before the arrival of an English army. The following year's raid met an expensive setback when Norham Castle, although badly damaged by the Scottish guns from across the Tweed, failed to fall. There, however, matters lay until the fateful year of 1513.

A DISASTROUS END IN 1513

The Scottish strategy in that year was not significantly different from the 1490s. All that had changed was the scale of operations and the reason for the attack. James invaded England in support of his French ally and hoped by so doing to draw English men and money away from the Continent. There is no reason to think that he intended, at least initially, to fight a pitched battle.

Another diversionary naval expedition was sent to Ireland to act in conjunction with the 'Wild Irish'. James had built up a navy, including the Michael, launched at Newhaven in 1511, arguably the largest ship afloat at the time. He also had commanders who had been successful in pitched battles at sea against the English. In the event, although the native Ulster leader O'Donnell was given two large guns and the royal fleet did attack Carrickfergus, this enterprise fizzled out.

James crossed over into England on 22 August with a large army and an impressive train of siege guns. Although a lot of the guns and gunners had been sent away on the ships the train was, as events proved, more than adequate for its task, and was accompanied by at least some gunners of experience. The army,

Berault Stuart, Seigneur d'Aubigny, dictating his treatise to his secretary, drawn from a 16th-century manuscript (Shepherd).

which may have started off with a strength of 30,000, was one of the largest ever gathered, reflecting James' popularity and effectiveness as a monarch.

James immediately set to against the fortresses of the East Marches. Norham fell in six days and the other major strongholds of Wark, Ford and Etal were also taken. Only the town and castle of Berwick remained untouched. Thus far James' expedition had been a great success, but he was in no hurry to leave. The host had been called out for a longer period than usual and he had been considerably bolstered by supplies of food, armaments and money from France. He had French military advisers with him, and very probably a copy of a treatise on warfare authored by a distant relative, Berault Stuart, Seigneur d'Aubigny, Marshall of France, one of the most experienced and respected soldiers of his day. He had dictated it just prior to succumbing to sickness on a visit to James in 1508. The enemy for once seemed surprisingly slow to materialise and James had to be sure that they would consider his efforts were worthy of more than a little attention.

When Henry VIII of England sailed for the Continent he had left the aged but experienced Earl of Surrey in command and he had the resources of all the northern shires to draw upon. The mechanisms for calling out their men were well oiled, and, together with a contingent from the English fleet under Surrey's son, Lord Thomas Howard, produced an army which on the field of battle was not much smaller than that of the Scots. What is more, unlike the Scottish, it was a professional army, with the soldiers being paid for

OPPOSITE: This ship, a representation of the Michael, is drawn from a pattern piece for a gold coin of James IV which shows the ship with the royal shield overlain in the centre (Shepherd).

ARMS PROCUREMENT

Much of the military equipment used by the Scots had to be imported from abroad, but the government did encourage local production, and foreign craftsmen to come and settle. James IV had Dutch firearms makers working in Edinburgh Castle from 1510. He also had French armourers to make luxury items unavailable from local armourers. Sword blades, including large ones for fashionable two-handed swords, were all imported, mostly from Germany, but they were mounted here by armourers with distinctive Scottish hilts. Scottish cutlers produced daggers, and bowyers manufactured not just bows but shafts for other weapons.

their services and being, by and large, experienced men.

Inexplicably, Surrey only called for the muster of his troops at Newcastle on 1 September, a week after the Scots invaded, and then only took the field at Bolton, near Alnwick, a good day, or at most two, away from the Scottish position at Ford on 3 September. Admittedly, the weather had turned excessively wet and stormy but the English response at this time was considerably slower than on other occasions, not from any lack of desire on Surrey's part to close with James. In fact his greatest fear was probably that he would miss the Scots altogether and have to explain away his vast expenditure on a futile exercise to his master Henry VIII. On 4 September Surrey shrewdly sent a challenge of battle to James – a challenge which James, if he wished to retain his prestige and self-respect, could not altogether ignore.

At the time he received Surrey's challenge James was at Ford and had probably been there for a number of days, perhaps like Surrey hampered by the bad weather. James sent a reply to Surrey that he would wait to do battle until Friday 9 September at noon, and took up a commanding position on Flodden Edge, within easy striking distance of the Border, fortifying it with earthworks.

FLODDEN

Surrey found, however, that he could flank the Scottish positions and hope to take the neighbouring Branxton Hill, thus cutting off the Scots from retreat over the Border. That Surrey intended this became clear to James by about 11 o'clock on the morning of the ninth, and in haste he struck camp and made to beat the enemy to Branxton Hill. This he achieved, grouping his army into four units to face the English. There was not sufficient time, however, to drag his heavy siege guns into place properly, and in the artillery dual with the lighter English fieldguns which preceded the main battle the Scots came off worst. They still, however, had the slope of the ground, sun and wind in their favour.

Surrey disposed his army in four units to match the Scots'. The English were a good 20,000 strong, all on foot, armed for the most part with bills, but bows and arrows as well. The bill was a long-shafted weapon with a fiercesome blade that could be used for chopping and stabbing.

The battle commenced about four or five in the afternoon. The English artillery fire precipitated James into ordering his army forward. All four battles advanced down the hill together, silently, in good order, with their pikes levelled. The English archers opened fire

A view of Flodden (Caldwell).

but were probably too few in number to have much effect on the well-armoured Scots.

On the Scots' left the battle led by Home and Huntly routed the opposing one under Edmund Howard, but two of the other Scottish battles were quickly broken up. The hardest fighting took place between the battles of the two commanders, and here it continued until nightfall, the Scots being pushed slowly and relentlessly back up the hill. James' men did not break, but in the clash their pikes ultimately proved less effective than the bills which were used to chop them into pieces.

As night fell (soon after six o'clock) the situation on the battlefield must have been something like this. On the Scots' left Hume and Huntly's battle remained intact, but Home, who was later made a scapegoat for the Scots' defeat, was unable to do anything as he was opposed by the English battle led by Lord Dacre. If either had turned to help in the fight between James and Surrey they would have been taken in flank and the victor would undoubtedly have swung the whole battle in their favour. Besides, both battles were largely composed of Borderers who may have been reluctant to fight each other. Time and again the Borderers were suspected of protecting their mutual interests in preference to supporting their own nation. One of the other two English units was by now well off, chasing the fugitives from the two broken Scottish battles, and the fourth was out of control, its men looting the dead.

When fighting ceased Surrey must have known that he had won, but it is probable that the full extent of his victory was not clear until the next day. After all, there were still large elements of the Scottish

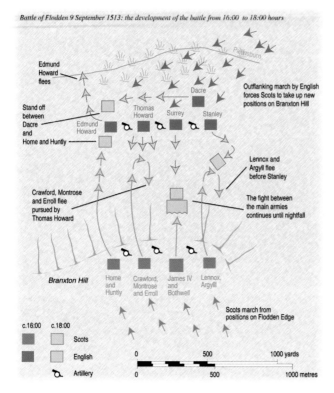

Battle of Flodden 9 September 1513: the development of the battle from 16:00 to 18:00 hours

Edmund Howard flees

Stand off between Dacre and Home and Huntly

Crawford, Montrose and Erroll flee pursued by Thomas Howard

Branxton Hill

Pallinsburn

Dacre

Thomas Howard   Surrey   Stanley

Edmund Howard

Outflanking march by English forces Scots to take up new positions on Branxton Hill

Lennox and Argyll flee before Stanley

The fight between the main armies continues until nightfall

Home and Huntly   Crawford, Montrose and Erroll   James IV and Bothwell   Lennox, Argyll

Scots march from positions on Flodden Edge

c.16:00   c.18:00

Scots

English

Artillery

0   500   1000 yards

0   500   1000 metres

host on the field, and one force even made an attempt the next day to rescue their artillery. The Scots, on the other hand, could not have doubted that all was lost, including their king and most of the leading nobles, struck down where they fought on foot in the front lines of their battles. James himself fell a spear's length from where Surrey stood. As many as 5,000 Scots may have died with him and 1,500 Englishmen.

THE LESSONS OF FLODDEN

Several reasons have been advanced for the Scots' defeat. A favourite explanantion is that the Scots were an amateur army facing professionals, attempting to copy a continental method of fighting without nearly enough training. It could also be argued that no amount of drilling would have mattered because their pikes had met their match in the English bills. Another point is that the leading ranks of the Scots were clad in armour and well armed, the nobles with swords, and many with targes as well. By contrast continental pikemen fought with practically no armour. Perhaps the weight of their equipment told against the Scots in the hard slugging match that ensued between the main battles. At least one English armourer, a certain William Tour, acquired large quantities of the defeated Scots' armour for resale. Over and above what he sold immediately after the battle he had 350 sets consisting of sallets (helmets), gorgets (neck pieces), backs, breasts and pairs of splints (for the arms).

Several factors may have contributed to the Scots' defeat but in saying so we are in danger of missing the point altogether. James should never have allowed himself to be drawn into a battle in the first place. He had successfully destroyed all the major castles of the East March, apart from Berwick, and had made sure the English had

From a contemporary English woodcut of Flodden. It shows Surrey being handed James IV's crown (Shepherd).

mobilised against him. Why throw it all away?

Far from learning from James' mistakes, the Regent Albany, who took over the reins of government in 1515, was determined to continue his military policies. Despite his distinguished career as a soldier in French service he found it difficult to motivate the Scots into risking another confrontation like Flodden. In 1522 he tried to lead an army through the West Marches but the Scots would not advance beyond the Border. In the following year, helped by French mercenaries, guns and some primitive tanks – carts mounted with guns, protected with metal, shields and sharp blades, drawn by barbed horses – he attempted the siege of Wark Castle on the Tweed, newly fortified with a great artillery tower. Again the Scots were reluctant and the weather unkind. Albany terminated the siege on news that an English relief army was near at hand. Soon after this failure he left Scotland for France, never to return.

Albany's expedition of 1523 marks the end of an era in Scottish warfare. It was the last major attempt by the Scots to win an advantage over the English by open assault and battery of their frontier fortifications. It was a strategy that looked as if it might promise good results in 1496, was disappointed in 1497 by the failure to take Norham Castle, and proved disastrous in 1513, 1522 and 1523. With the notable exception of 1542, the Scots remained on the defensive in fighting with the English for the rest of the century. The reliance of Albany on French mercenaries at the siege of Wark was a sign of things to come.

CHAPTER 6

FAILURE – OR ULTIMATE SUCCESS IN 1603?

FRANCE AND ENGLAND COMPETE FOR SCOTLAND

Militarily, the 16th century was a time when the Scots failed to keep up in the arms race and became the prize for the two competing powers, France and England. The latter were the clear winners in 1560 when French forces were forced to withdraw from Scotland. In 1603 Scotland and England were united under the Scottish king, James VI.

The Wars of the Rough Wooing (1547-50) saw the Scots play a subsidiary role in their own country as the French and English spent massively to win the marriage of the young Mary Queen of Scots. French and English armies were sent to Scotland on several occasions from 1545 to 1573 in support of one Scottish faction or another. The Scots did retain their military traditions and did all in their power to remain an effective fighting force. What they principally lacked was not courage or resolve, but money for equipment and trained personnel. The Scottish war machine had been ideally suited for low budget defence of the country against the English but failed in the 16th century to develop into a creditable deterrent in campaigns fought in all seasons against professional armies based in fortifications.

OPPOSITE: Tantallon Castle, East Lothian. The massive 14th-century curtain walls withstood James V's guns in 1528 (Historic Scotland).

Mary the Queen, centre and cause of the Wars of Rough wooing; profile drawn from a gold ryal or £3 piece (Shepherd).

63

TRACE ITALIENNE FORTIFICATIONS

Trace italienne fortifications were the answer to the new destructive power of guns. As the name suggests they were developed in Italy at the turn of the 16th century and were soon being designed all over Europe, principally by Italian engineers. Typically they had a solid earth rampart, only the top of which protruded above a massive ditch. They were thus a difficult target for enemy guns. At regular intervals on the circuit of the rampart they had large angular bastions, placed in such a way that guns in positions in the flanks of the bastions could fire along the fronts of the adjacent ramparts and bastions. Other guns were mounted to fire out over the defences to the country beyond the fort. In the more permanent forts, like the ones erected by the French in the years from 1548 to 1560 at Leith, Dunbar, Inchkeith and Eyemouth, the defences were faced in stonework for greater strength.

In the Wars of the Rough Wooing several trace italienne forts were built by the English and French. The English, under the Protector Somerset, invaded Scotland in September 1547. They hoped to create a 'pale', an area dominated by forts, where the Scots would be persuaded to co-operate with them. The Scottish Government would thus be forced into a marriage alliance, allowing their young queen to marry the young Edward VI. In hindsight it is easy to judge that the policy was fatally flawed, not least because the French were not prepared to let the English steal such a prize from their ally. Indeed they had already intervened in Scotland militarily on behalf of the Scottish Government in 1545 and 1547.

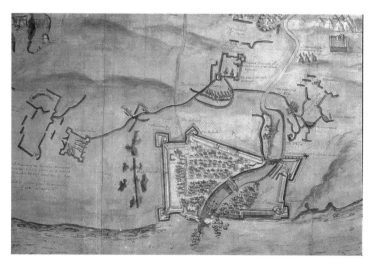

The port of Leith, as fortified by the French by 1560, with enormous earthwork ramparts and bastions. This English view also shows the English siegeworks (by kind permission of Lord Egremont).

Trace italienne fortifications 1547-60

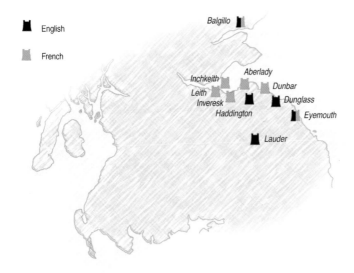

In June 1548 a French expeditionary force, 10,000 strong, comprising mostly Swiss and German mercenaries, arrived at Leith, and was soon challenging the English. The only major battle of the war was at Pinkie in September 1547 between the Scots and English. The rest of the hostilities revolved around the English forts, especially their main base at Haddington, but also at Broughty and Lauder. From November 1548 the English were almost totally on the defensive. When they finally gave up in March 1550 they only retained the forts at Lauder, then under siege, Eyemouth, and a fort constructed in the ruins of Roxburgh Castle. Nevertheless, the only one of the new forts which had fallen to direct assault was the English fort at Broughty (Balgillo) near Dundee. Haddington had survived a siege of many months and two major attempts by French and Scottish forces to storm its ramparts. Its garrison finally marched out because the English Government no longer had the resolve or the resources to maintain it.

The best preserved of these forts is at Eyemouth on the Berwickshire coast. The fortification of it was commenced by the English in September 1547. The site is a promontory and the English engineer, Sir Richard Lee, only considered it necessary to put a rampart across the neck of the headland, with one centrally-placed, arrowhead-shaped bastion. While the ditch and rampart could be raked with fire from gun positions in the flanks of the bastion, the

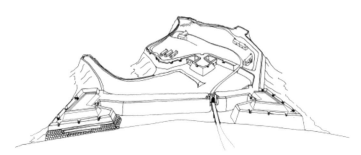

Present view and a reconstruction drawing of the Fort at Eyemouth, Berwickshire, immediately prior to its demolition in 1559. The inner line of defences with the central bastion was built by the English in 1547 and remodelled by the French. The outer line, still unfinished, was commenced by the French in 1557 (reconstruction by Leonie Paterson).

bastion could only be covered by guns set in casemates in the rampart itself. This was a design weakness in that it would have been relatively easy for besieging guns to target and dismount the casemate guns.

A 16th-century gun embrasure for a small piece of artillery at Ravenscraig Castle, Fife (Caldwell).

The English dismantled Eyemouth in the summer of 1551, but the site was reoccupied by the French in 1557 who started to build a larger and more sophisticated fort. The main defensive line was better positioned and had two large bastions to support each other. Their earthworks were faced in stone for greater permanence. These fortifications were pulled down in 1559 but their outline can still be traced on the ground today.

Despite the example of the

English and French, the Scots were reluctant to adopt the new fortifications. Many castles were provided with gun-loops, even if just for show, and there are a few interesting experiments in castle building in the century, which take account of the destructive effect of artillery, but little evidence for serious earthwork forts. The reason is perhaps best expressed in a document of 1560 recommending the demolition of all the fortifications made or begun in the previous ten years. It says that histories and experience had taught the Scots that fortresses had never preserved the country from invasions and that the main reason that Scotland had so long remained a free nation was the lack of them since an enemy finding no place to lodge himself could only burn a small part of the country before departing.

THE SIEGE OF TANTALLON, 1528

Scottish governments of the period were certainly more interested in capturing fortifications than maintaining them. Their ability to do so with their own resources was a measure of the country's military competence. The well-documented siege of Tantallon Castle in 1528 (frontispiece to this chapter) was an early warning of what could go wrong.

The young king, James V, on taking personal control of government in 1528, was determined to be revenged on the Earl of Angus, the head of the Douglases, for keeping him a virtual prisoner for several years. Angus ravished Lothian and James was driven off after trying to take Coldingham Priory in Berwickshire. On 7 September he ordered a complete call out of the host at Edinburgh for 20 October to go and besiege Tantallon Castle near North Berwick, Angus' chief stronghold and undoubtedly one of the strongest fortresses in the land. It had a great 14th-century curtain wall, over 3.6m (nearly 12 ft) thick, with a deep rock-cut ditch in front of it. The hosting was only to be for 20 days, probably the most James could then keep his army together.

The real strength of his army should have been in its artillery, but here there were major problems to be overcome. Scotland was still struggling to re-arm and replace all the guns lost at Flodden, and James had to borrow some guns from Albany's garrison in Dunbar Castle. Even so, his artillery train, with no more than six large guns (cannons), three medium-sized pieces (culverin bastards) and some smaller guns, was a rather meagre battery for the task in hand. A worse problem by far was the lack of powder and shot. James was evidently relying on borrowing powder from some of his subjects. In the event some powder left by the exiled Danish king, Christian II,

ARMS AND ARMOUR

A significant development, perhaps as a result of lessons learned at Flodden, was the almost complete abandonment of head-to-foot plate armour in favour of lighter jacks and brigandines, worn together with simple iron hats (with a variety of different names). Swords, single and two-handed versions, were becoming increasingly available, and pistols and guns. Long-shafted axes remained popular, as did bows and arrows amongst the Highlanders. Throughout this period, however, the main units of the host continued to fight on foot as pike formations, marshalled in great battles composed of rows and columns of men, as deep as they were broad.

as security for debts with Robert Barton, the famous merchant and sea captain, was purloined for the siege. His chief gunners had only recommended 30 pieces of shot per gun, although a cannon at that time might be expected to shoot 40 times a day. Were they influenced in their assessment by knowlege of what was available?

Things did not go well at Tantallon for the king. The castle was bombarded in vain for several days with no damage being done to the defenders, but several of the besiegers were killed, wounded and burned by the explosion of a powder magazine. James gave up the siege on 4 November with nothing achieved, leaving a band of foot and a company of horse to bring home the artillery. That night Angus issued out with a body of 160 horse, attacked and defeated those remaining, killing their captain, David Falconer, a favourite of the king, and taking prisoner the master of the artillery, Sir Alexander Jardine. Angus wrote to the English that not to dishonour the king he conducted the artillery out of danger and released Jardine, praying him to tell James that he had been his true servant; but according to

The early 17th-century stone carvings in Edinburgh Castle showing guns and munitions of the 16th century (Shepherd).

James, Angus did take some of his guns, and he certainly never forgave him for the slaughter of Falconer.

James V's siege of Tantallon Castle was a failure. Unlike the expeditions of James IV against the English border fortresses, lack of time was not such a crucial element. Lack of equipment probably was, and a certain amount of disorganisation among the professional gunners, wrights, smiths, and others who looked after the artillery. Jardine, who had just been reinstated as master of the artillery a matter of weeks before the siege (after a spell when the Douglases had intruded their own protege), immediately lodged a protest with the Lords of Council that he should not be held responsible for the poor state of the guns. The powder explosion during the siege does not reflect highly on the efficiency of the operation.

James V never learnt from his mistakes at Tantallon, and a glorious military career was not for him. His tactless handling of his nobility led to what amounted to a revolt on the field of battle in 1542, when, in an engagement with the English at Solway Moss, many deliberately gave themselves up without a fight.

THE SUCCESSES AND FAILURES OF GOVERNOR ARRAN

James Hamilton, Earl of Arran, who governed Scotland on the death of James V in 1542, seemed at first to have remarkable success in siegework. The list of castles that fell is quite impressive: Dalkeith in 1543, Glasgow in 1544, Caerlaverock and Lochmaben in 1545, and Dumbarton in 1546. What is more, Arran seems to have had access to even fewer siege guns than James V in 1528. With due humility he wrote to the Pope that he had recovered Dumbarton Castle by a miracle.

Then it was the turn of St Andrews Castle in Fife, being held by the murderers of Cardinal Beaton. A tax was granted by the clergy for

Aerial view of Caerlaverock Castle (Historic Scotland).

FOOD AND SUPPLIES

When the host was summoned each man had to supply his own equipment, food, and fodder for his horse. At the end of the Middle Ages it was not expected that the army would live off the land, either in Scotland or England. The effort of organising well-provisioned men with separate baggage trains of pack horses would have fallen on the officials and noblemen who led the contingents from each lordship or shire. When the Regent Moray made an expedition in 1568 against Border reivers his fighting force of 4,000 horse and 1,000 foot was accompanied by 4,000 carriage horse with 3,000 boys and young men. Sometimes, in return for not sending their own men, the burghs were ordered to provide food and drink for sale.

its siege in August 1546 and Arran arranged for the host to muster quarter by quarter for 20 days at a time.

Arran's son was being held a hostage within the castle and it was this, as much as the fact that it was one of the strongest in Scotland, newly fortified with two great circular blockhouses, well provisioned, and held by resolute, experienced men, that influenced the governor to try and gain it by mining. By late October he is said to have mined almost to the foot of the tower. The defenders, however, were aware of this work and were already countermining and showing no great fear. Mine and countermine survive to this day, hewn out of the solid rock. They show that the castilians must have been successful in heading off the governor's attempt, thus forcing him to try and do a deal with them. The castilians refused his offer of Blackness Castle, restitution and a full pardon in return for his son and the castle, and Arran launched an artillery barrage with renewed vigour at the end of November. A report from those inside the castle describes how the guns shot continuously, battering the roofs and battlements and spoiling a month's provisions in the cellar and brewhouse. This bombardment only lasted two days and Arran had to abandon the siege on 17 December for lack of powder and shot. His son was released safely when the castle was captured by the French.

Undeterred by his failure at St Andrews, Arran set off the following summer to besiege Langholm Castle, a tower-house of the Maxwells in Dumfries-shire which had recently had an English garrison installed in it. The whole host was called out for the task and Arran sent his guns, some by Peebles and others by Lauder, to keep the English guessing as long as possible about his true intentions. The tower is said to have withstood several cannon shots, but no sooner had it fallen than word came of the arrival at St Andrews of a French fleet under the command of Leon Strozzi, the Prior of Capua.

The eye-witness account of John Knox, the subsequently renowned Protestant reformer, then one of the castle garrison, relates how Strozzi had ten cannons and four double cannons. On the first day they were planted in position, it took a bombardment of less than six hours for the castle to be beaten into submission. Knox and his companions were taken off to France to serve as galley slaves. Meanwhile the Scottish guns, dragged in haste from Langholm, had still not arrived.

Perhaps it is unkind to compare the Scots' failure over several months at St Andrews with Strozzi's incisive, well-equipped assault of a few hours. Contemporaries certainly did, and drew the conclusion that the Scots were militarily weak, unable to operate in a new military environment that demanded expensive equipment and

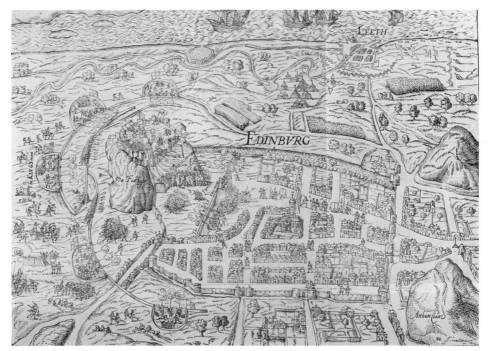

skilled operators. St Andrews Castle by European standards was a tough nut to crack, but Scotland was peppered with tower-houses like Langholm. The whole of the country's fighting force for several days seems a disproportionate effort to have to expend on such an inconvenience.

For the rest of the 16th century Scottish governments mostly had to rely on others to provide guns to do their work for them. In the Wars of the Rough Wooing it was the French. In 1560 for the siege of Leith, in 1570 for destroying the power of the Hamiltons, in 1573 for the siege of Edinburgh Castle, and in 1587 for the siege of Lochmaben Castle, it was the English. After the Union of the Crowns siege trains could even be brought from Dublin, as for expeditions to Islay in 1608 and 1615.

An English view of the successful siege of Edinburgh Castle in 1573. The castle was the last to be held for Mary Queen of Scots. Note the gun batteries surrounding the castle and the assault taking place on its forework (from a 19th-century facsimile of Holinshed's Chronicle).

SCOTTISH PROWESS

The major pitched battle of the period, indeed the last between Scotland and England as separate countries, was an unedifying disaster for the Scots. It took place at Pinkie on 'Black Saturday' 10 September, 1547. English intelligence reports had predicted that the Scottish governor, the Earl of Arran, would be unable to put together an army to oppose their invasion. In the event Arran fielded one of

Contemporary drawings of the Battle of Pinkie, 10 September 1547, from a book by William Patten, who served in the English Army. Left: the two armies advance to battle. Right: the Scots drop their weapons and turn and flee.
Key:
A: the English camp
B, C, D: the English foot
E: an enclosure
F: the bottom of the hill
G: the Duke of Somerset
H: the English artillery
I: the English horse
K: a ditch
L: a lane flanked by turf walls
M, N, O: the Scottish foot
P, P: hillocks
Q: Inveresk Church
R: Musselburgh
S: the Scottish horse
TTTT: the Scottish camp
V: a turf wall protecting the Scottish camp on the sea-side
W: the English baggage train
X: a marsh
Y: an English galley
Z: Edinburgh Castle

the strongest Scottish armies ever, about 22,000 or 23,000 men. They fought, as at Flodden, in large battles with pikes. They saw off an initial assault by the English horse but broke and fled before the main forces could come together, leaving 6,000 dead and 2,000 prisoner.

The sudden panic that seized the Scots was the predictable result of trying to turn a mass of amateurs into a professional army. Drill work, which the modern army recruit finds difficult enough on the parade ground, the Scot of the 16th century had to learn on the field of battle with disastrous results.

An interesting lesson the Scots do seem to have learnt from Pinkie was the importance of guns, particularly hand-guns. It was the annoyance from these which more than anything precipitated their flight. There were few Scots armed with hand-guns at Pinkie, but as the century progressed more and more of those who could afford to do so armed themselves with long guns or pistols, many made by craftsmen in the towns, particularly Edinburgh and Dundee. Culverins and pistols played a part in the battle at Langside, near Glasgow in 1568 between the supporters of Mary Queen of Scots and the Regent Moray.

Fortunately, the Scots continued to demonstrate their skill and prowess in innumerable cross-border raids, with forces only a few hundred strong. In small-scale battles, under good leadership, they could acquit themselves admirably in hand-to-hand fighting, as against the English at Lilliard's Edge (Ancrum) in 1545. There were many reasons why the English were prepared to accept a Scottish

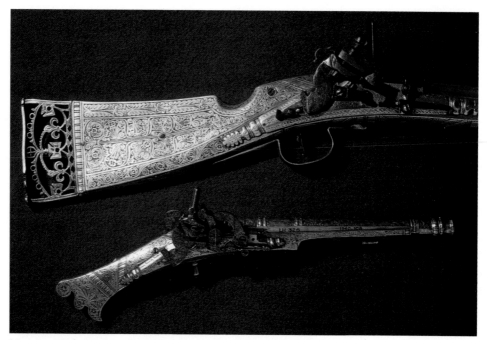

king in 1603. High among them was the realisation that after 400 years they had failed to conquer their northern neighbour or create peace and security in their own Borders. Perhaps the Union of the Crowns should be viewed as the ultimate success of Scottish military abilities.

A gun and pistol of brass made in Dundee in 1611 by James Low. The pistol belonged to Louis XIII of France. By the late 16th century the Scots were aware of the importance of firearms and several of their own craftsmen were supplying the need (National Museums of Scotland).

A wood carving of c. 1600, said to have come from a bed in Threave Castle. This detail shows a soldier of the period armed with a gun (National Museums of Scotland).

CHAPTER 7

COVENANTERS AND ROYALISTS

MILITIA AND HIGHLAND ARMIES IN THE MID 17TH CENTURY

The Union of Scotland and England in 1603 did not see the end of warfare in Britain, and in the civil wars of the mid 17th century Scottish armies were again to be pitted against English forces. These wars were about religion and the struggle between king and parliament. They affected everyone in all the countries of the British Isles, and involved a bewildering number of campaigns, alliances and changes of allegiance for many of the principle players.

OPPOSITE: *Basket-hilted sword, targe and pistol - mainstays of the armoury of the Highland Armies in the 17th century (National Museums of Scotland).*

In Scotland the discontent of many was focused upon the attempt by Charles I to impose bishops, and hence greater royal authority, on a staunchly presbyterian church. Those who resisted the king became known as covenanters, after their national covenant - manifesto - drawn up in 1638. The king's supporters were called royalists. At first the covenanters were in league with the king's enemies in England - the parliamentarians ('Roundheads') - but this alliance fell apart in 1648, leading to a new phase in the conflict with Scottish armies opposing the English, led by Oliver Cromwell.

In the years from 1639 to 1647 Scottish armies were again a force to be reckoned with. They won pitched battles in Scotland and England, besieged and captured English towns, and occupied the whole north of England. There were, however, two very different types of army, militia and Highland. The militia armies were created by Alexander Leslie (created Earl of Leven in 1641); the Highland armies are associated with the Marquis of Montrose and Alasdair MacColla.

RAISING THE MILITIA

In military matters, the brief turn in Scotland's fortunes away from the low point reached in the 16th century was largely due to the establishment of a militia army, conceived and led by Scottish officers with experience of the continental wars, and administered both nationally and at a local level by an effective system of committees. It is remarkable that this should have been developed despite, indeed against, royal authority.

In the years from 1639 to 1651 the Scots raised several armies, 20,000 men strong, and kept them in the field for months – even years – at a time, on active service in England. An army of 10,000 was sent to Ireland in 1642 and several smaller forces were also campaigning in Scotland.

In the late 16th and early 17th century there was a great outpouring of Scots to France, the Low Countries and the lands round the Baltic, many going purposely to take up arms, particularly in the service of King Gustavus Adolphus of Sweden, an outstanding military thinker and strategist. It is said that some 10,000 Scots served in his army, and one of them, Robert Monro, knew of over 100 Scottish officers who held Swedish commissions in 1632, besides several of lesser rank. The army of the Solemn League and Covenant raised by the Scots in 1643 had 55 out of 92 senior officers with experience of continental warfare. The rest were drawn from the ranks of the nobility.

Most important in the former group was Alexander Leslie, one of the most competent soldiers of his age, having risen to the rank of field-marshall in the Swedish army. A contemporary writer, Robert Baillie, tells how much help and advice was got from him in preparing to put the country on a war footing, and many of the decisions taken by the small group of leading covenanters who met in Edinburgh and effectively took over the governance of the country are best explained as the result of access to his considerable military expertise.

German woodcut of 1631 showing Highlanders in Swedish service.

National sentiment and lack of money meant that an army of mercenaries, such as many countries had come to rely on, was out of the question. The obvious alternative was to call out the host, relying on the great men to organise and lead their own contingents as for ages past. This method of raising the fencibles was by no means moribund, but had been little used for some time. Instead, the covenanters, as in other areas of administration,

embarked on a new course, by raising a militia army of paid men, pressed to serve. It was no coincidence that the successful Swedish army was also of this type.

A committee of war in each shire was responsible for levying men, munitions, food and money for the army. Through commissioners in the parishes they were able to choose the appropriate number of men and

ensure that the country was not depleted of essential workers. From the beginning the covenanters saw clearly that they would have to be prepared to keep their forces in the field longer than the traditional 40 days at a stretch, and the troops would have to be paid, not just wages but billet money or subsistence as well. The raising of taxes was an answer to this problem.

Alexander Leven and other allied commanders, drawn from the contemporary engraving by Richard Clampe of the siegeworks at Newark On Trent, 1645 (Shepherd).

Leslie knew full well that it was not enough to find the men and the money for an army and to him more than anyone else must go the credit for devising means of forming an effective fighting force. He took it upon himself to make contact with other Scottish professional soldiers serving on the Continent, and to encourage their return. He saw to the gathering of supplies of munitions and may have been responsible for the short treatise on the Rudiments of Military Discipline published in Edinburgh in 1638. This contained basic instructions on how to handle pikes and muskets and how to exercise bodies of soldiers, and was obviously intended as a manual to be used in drilling new recruits and the fencibles at the wapinschawings.

ORGANISING AND TRAINING THE MILITIA

The army formed under Leslie's watchful eye was in marked contrast to the medieval host. Now it was split up into manageable regiments on a territorial (shire by shire) basis. These regiments could vary considerable in size, and were normally smaller than the ideal of 1,000 men. There were several ranks of officers, creating an effective chain of command, and to a large extent these officers owed their positions to their ability rather than status as landowners.

There was greater uniformity in weapons and their specifications - for the foot, limited to either pike or musket. Muskets by this time

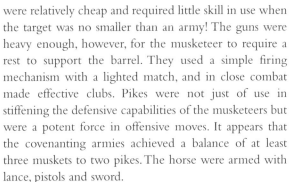

were relatively cheap and required little skill in use when the target was no smaller than an army! The guns were heavy enough, however, for the musketeer to require a rest to support the barrel. They used a simple firing mechanism with a lighted match, and in close combat made effective clubs. Pikes were not just of use in stiffening the defensive capabilities of the musketeers but were a potent force in offensive moves. It appears that the covenanting armies achieved a balance of at least three muskets to two pikes. The horse were armed with lance, pistols and sword.

In general the Scots seem to have worn little armour or protective clothing. Some had steel breast and back plates but jacks and 'buffil' coats, made of stout leather, were more common for body defence while bonnets, incorporating a steel cap, were the favoured covering for the head. None of the Scottish armies of the period had a uniform as we would understand it today, but the troops were supplied with footware and clothing, typically of grey cloth, and it was normal practice for armies to adopt identifying badges and slogans just prior to an engagement.

Musketeers preparing and firing; they were an important element in the militia armies. The muskets were heavy and required a rest for firing them (from F. Grose, Military Antiquities).

In battle the army was divided into brigades of two or three regiments to make effective use of all its manpower rather than rely on the weight of massed ranks pressing forward from behind. These brigades, normally less than 2,000 men strong, were more manoeuvrable than the battles of the previous century. A greater proportion of men was brought into the sharp end of the conflict, and within reasonable earshot and sight of their commanders, by the brigades being drawn up no more than six, or as few as four, rows deep. Perhaps most significant was the great emphasis placed on discipline and drill, the twin anchors of modern armies. The desire for all these improved features was not lacking in earlier times but now with professional officers and a militia army, all were possible and to a large extent achieved.

Cavalry was raised in troops, theoretically 60 strong, which were then grouped into regiments. The army of the Solemn League and Covenant had eight regiments, amounting to 3,000 horse in all, and a regiment of dragoons, that is mounted infantry, 500 to 600 strong.

There was also the artillery, to which the Scots paid a lot of attention. Gustavus Adolphus had pioneered the development of the light field gun for his brilliant campaigns in Europe in the 1620s and 1630s, and two of his Scottish officers, Alexander Hamilton and James Wemyss, were influential in introducing Swedish ideas to Scotland. The main principle was to have guns which were light enough to be easily manoeuvred and fired on the field of battle without notably sacrificing their strength and power. Hamilton had short bronze field guns which fired cartridges of grape-shot and multi-barrelled guns mounted in a wooden frame which could be carried on horseback.

A cavalryman. The cavalry of the militia armies relied on pistols and were not always very effective (from F Grose, Military Antiquities).

Wemyss was responsible for manufacturing leather guns from his appointment in 1649, and remarkably, several of his pieces survive. They are of very light construction with short barrels mostly mounted on axle-bars in groups of two, three or four. Each barrel is made of a sheet of thin iron bent into a tube secured by iron rings shrunk and riveted into place. The barrels were then tightly wound with hemp

A leather gun, the work of James Wemyss, c. 1650. Most of the leather and cord has rotted away, exposing the wrought-iron cores of the barrels (Caldwell).

cord and covered with a leather coat. This method of construction gave just enough strength for the gun to fire two or three rounds of grape-shot or stone balls.

ALEXANDER LESLIE AS COMMANDER, 1639-1647

Leslie knew the weaknesses of his army. No amount of drill and training, or officers with continental service, could make up for its lack of experience. He was rightly reluctant to expose his army to the chance of battle except in the most favourable of circumstances, as at Newburn in 1640. To gain Newcastle he had to cross the River Tyne and take it from the south where it was less well defended. He found the royalist commander Conway protecting the crossing with 4,000 men and guns and protective earthworks, but the covenanters, in one of the few effective artillery bombardments of the wars, were easily able to outgun their opponents and their superior numbers were more than a match for Conway's men.

Leslie, however, also appreciated the strength of his army. In that it existed at all it was a potent weapon that could paralyse large tracts of disaffected or enemy country and tie down enemy troops. The longer it remained in arms the more it wore down the opposition since it was paid and quartered at English expense. In 1639, while the greater part of Scotland backed the covenanting cause, King Charles had great difficulty in keeping an army in the field to oppose them since the English Parliament would not supply him with money. Leslie was thus able to tighten the screw, moving his forces from Dunglass to Duns to apply more pressure to the royal army encamped a few miles away at Berwick while at the same time avoiding conflict. It is likely that, thanks to Scottish bluff and propaganda, Charles believed that the Scots army was bigger than it actually was.

In the years from 1644 to 1646 much of the covenanting army's time was taken up with besieging the enemy towns of York, Newcastle and Newark, but in the actual campaigning in the countryside and the one major battle at Marston Moor Leslie - now Earl of Leven - showed his skill in using the lie of the land to his advantage. As his army moved south from Newcastle in March 1644 it was followed by a royalist army under the Marquess of Newcastle, but Leven, by choosing his ground carefully, was able to see the enemy off without a fight and occupy Sunderland.

A Scottish siege work at Newark, drawn from Clampe's plan of the siegeworks in 1645 (Shepherd).

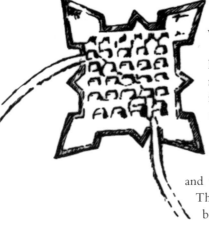

Newcastle, now joined by the Scottish royalist leader Montrose, was determined to stop Leven making contact with the English parliamentary forces further south. On 24 March he drew up his army at Hylton to the west of Sunderland to block the covenanters' progress, but Leven was too cautious a general to risk his men on unfavourable ground not of his own choosing and was content to await an attack by the royalists. There was much skirmishing and a cannon bombardment that lasted well into the night, and the next day there was a cavalry engagement, all of which were indecisive. Newcastle, however, failed in his objective of stopping the Scots and withdrew to Durham.

Leven was not always so keen to avoid battle as was seen at Marston Moor, outside York, a few weeks later on 2 July, where his allied army of Scots covenanters and English parliamentary forces confronted the combined royalist army of Prince Rupert and Newcastle. Rupert had just relieved the siege of York, and Leven's tasks were clearly to prevent the prince breaking through to the south to aid the king, and to take York once and for all. At Marston both achievements were in his grasp.

Leven had under his command his own Scottish forces, and two English armies led by Lords Fairfax and Manchester. He deployed his forces along the crest of a ridge facing the royalist army at a distance of about half a mile beyond a ditch. The two armies were probably fairly evenly matched in terms of numbers at between 18 and 19,000 each. Accounts vary but it seems that the foot was divided into 14 brigades, nine of them Scottish, and these brigades were drawn up in three lines, one behind the other. The horse were placed on the wings, and Leven seems to have deliberately made his left wing stronger by placing his best cavalry there. It was commanded by two officers who were later to achieve great fame, both individually and as opponents - the Englishman, Oliver Cromwell, and the Scotsman, David Leslie (no relation of Leven).

Both armies were drawn up by about two o'clock in the afternoon and there were some shots of artillery from both sides which caused little damage. Rupert, who had been discouraged from forcing battle by his colleagues, eventually decided that Leven was not going to

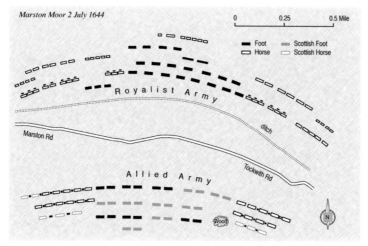

Marston Moor 2 July 1644

fight in earnest that day. Leven, perceiving the royalists were intent on settling down for the night, ordered the allied army forward about seven o'clock in the evening to gain some advantage of surprise.

The Scottish dragoons cleared the enemy musketeers from the ditch, thus allowing Cromwell and David Leslie's horse across safely. While they went on to defeat the royalists' right wing of cavalry, reinforced by Rupert with his reserves, the allies' right wing was scattered and much of the foot faired badly. Several Scottish regiments in the rear fled precipitately as the defeated cavalry of Lord Fairfax returned in disorder, trampling some of them down. Only Manchester's foot on the left, under a Scottish officer, Lawrence Crawford, and some of the Scottish regiments on the right under Baillie and Lumsden, stood their ground, the Scots pressed all the while by the victorious royalist cavalry who had captured the allied guns and moved round to plunder their supply train. Meantime, Leven and Fairfax left the field believing that all was lost.

At this critical juncture, after the remaining Scots foot, five and a bit regiments in all, had been fending off the enemy cavalry for the space of about an hour, the allies' horse under Cromwell and David Leslie reappeared and, driving off the royalist cavalry, delivered the winning blow. The allied foot and horse together were then able to turn their attentions to the royalist foot, and by the time complete darkness fell it was clear they had thoroughly beaten them. Newcastle's command was totally destroyed and Rupert's remaining forces were scattered. The official report of the allied generals speaks of 3,000 enemy dead on the field and 1,500 prisoners with only 200 or 300 losses of their own.

Leven's skill in drawing up the army is not in doubt, nor his judgement in timing the attack. The battle was one of the largest on British soil in this period and meant the loss of the whole of the north of England, except Newcastle, to King Charles. It is interesting to note that at a later date the parliamentarians looked back to Marston Moor, wistfully remembering the harmony between the commanders. But such goodwill as there was between the Scots and English received a rude blow in the immediate aftermath of the battle thanks to the way it was reported. The Scots felt they were denied full credit by the English for their part in it.

Leven himself seems to have lived down his untimely flight. He returned north to Newcastle, and took it by assault on 19 October after a long hard siege. Despite the toughness of the fighting and the refusal of the town to surrender there was no massacre of the population and little looting.

THE ROYALIST CAMPAIGN UNDER MONTROSE

Meanwhile the royalist cause in Scotland had life breathed into it by the arrival of Alasdair MacColla, of the Clan Donald, in June 1644, bringing from Ireland a force of 2,000 experienced Irish soldiers. MacColla came together with the appointed royalist commander in Scotland, James Graham, Marquis of Montrose, and soon they had an army of about 5,000 under their command, composed almost entirely of Highlanders and Irishmen. They embarked on a remarkable, year-long campaign in Scotland, achieving victory over covenanting armies in six pitched battles: at Tibbermore near Perth on 1 September 1644, at Aberdeen on 13 September, Inverlochy on 2 February 1645, Auldearn on 9 May, Alford on 2 July, and Kilsyth on 15 August. Only at Alford was their army not seriously outnumbered: at Auldearn it was by as much as two to one.

The Marquis of Montrose, image drawn from a contemporary portrait (Shepherd).

The Highlanders in this royalist army fought in clan units. Indeed the whole of traditional Highland society was organised for war. The main asset of any chief was not his land or animals but his men. The tacksmen (leaseholders), often close kinsmen of the chief, naturally took the role of officers over their tenants. Men were inured to war from an early age and their powers of endurance and ability to march fast were consistently remarked upon with astonishment.

THE HIGHLAND CHARGE

The whole-hearted adoption of the broadsword and targe together with their scanty, light-weight dress allowed for the adoption of a tactic in warfare known to us today as the Highland Charge. This use of a broadsword with a targe was unique to the Highlanders. The targe, or target, a circular, leather covered, wooden shield held on the lower arm as a body defence, has a very long history, but was typically employed in conjunction with a spear or an axe. Targes were made by their own craftsmen from readily available materials. The broadsword, fitted with a basket hilt for complete protection of the hand, was ideal for slashing. By the mid 17th century swords were cheap enough to be carried by most fighting men.

Before commencing the attack, the Highlanders, like athletes, stripped off their outer clothes and shoes, and advanced to battle at a trot. When a few metres from the enemy, they paused to fire their muskets. These were then thrown aside and a final dash made on the

The civil wars 1639 to 1651

Auldeam
6 May 1645

Alford
2 July 1645

Aberdeen
13 Sept 1644

Inverlochy
2 Feb 1645

Tippermuir
1 Sept 1644

Kilsyth
15 Aug 1645

Philiphaugh
13 Sept 1645

All these battles were resounding victories for Montrose, apart from the last, at Philiphaugh

opposing lines. Targes caught the opposing pikes or bayonets while swords hacked through bodies unprotected by armour. Many Highlanders also had dirks and pistols as a final option for close quarter fighting. The armies which had to withstand the shock of the Highland charge were composed of drilled, militia or professional soldiers, who were taught to move slowly and deliberately, to stand their ground, to hold their fire and shoot in unison. On other battle fields, against other enemies, the same men withstood volleys of lead and marched on enemy guns; but faced with men they regarded as savages, who ran at them before they had time to reload, and who wielded blades which sliced through heads and limbs, they invariably broke and fled within minutes.

The question arises as to how the Highland charge originated. The best explanation is that it was introduced by Alasdair MacColla. He had experience of fighting in Ireland. At the battle of the Laney in 1642, in which a party of British from Coleraine were ambushed and soundly beaten by a native Irish grouping including MacColla

Targe, broadsword and dirk, the weapons for delivering the Highland Charge (National Museums of Scotland).

and a force of MacDonnells, he is said to have commanded his men to lay down their firearms and then fall upon the British with their swords and dirks. Targes were also in use in Ireland at that time.

Tibbermore is the classic encounter. The covenanters had underestimated the speed of Montrose's advance and the seriousness of the threat. There were no experienced militia regiments available and it was thus a hastily gathered army of the fencibles from Fife and Perthshire, 6,000 foot and 700 horse, lacking its appointed commander, the Earl of Lothian, which confronted the royalists on the morning of 1 September. The overall command was delegated to Lord Elcho who personally led the battalion on the right. He had two others, that in the centre under the command of Sir James Scott, the only senior officer with any experience, and the left hand battalion under the Earl of Tullibardine. The horse, led by Lord Drummond was placed on the wings and there were seven pieces of artillery planted in front of the line.

Montrose lacked both horse and artillery and had to draw out his force, perhaps only 2,400 strong at this point, to avoid being outflanked by the covenanters. The two battalions on the wings were thus only three ranks deep. Those on the left were local levies, mostly archers, under Lord Kilpont and Sir John Drummond, and on the right were men raised in Badenoch and Atholl. The main strength of the army lay in the three regiments of experienced Irish and Islesmen, brigaded in the centre. They were described as musketeers and were led by Alasdair MacColla. Montrose may have led the right wing, fighting on foot with target and pike. Montrose had acquitted himself well in the wars, first on the covenanting side and then with the royalists in England. Now at Tibbermore his task seemed clear. An enemy army in front and another led by Argyll not far behind, he had to win a decisive victory not only to survive but to give his campaign any chance of gaining momentum.

It was the covenanters, however, who opened hostilities by sending out some foot and horse under Lord Drummond to skirmish with the royalists as they edged southwards from Newbigging to gain the advantage of rising ground. They were driven off with surprising ease by some troops detailed for the purpose by Montrose, and a full scale counter-attack was immediatley launched. Alasdair MacColla's men sped forward, fired and jettisoned their muskets, and were quickly upon the covenanters with their swords and dirks despite the artillery and an attempt by the cavalry to take them in flank and rear. Stones picked from the ground proved of some help in warding off the horse.

The Highlanders on the right wing imitated the Irish, but whereas the main body of the enemy gave back as soon as Alasdair MacColla was upon them, here James Scott persuaded his men to offer a little resistance before they too fled. The slaughter was enormous as Montrose failed to keep his men from the pursuit, for as much as six or seven miles. At least 1,500 are said to have been killed and 200 taken prisoner.

Tibbermore contains all the elements which made for Montrose's success. In the first place was the speed of his march, and secondly, the effective use of the Highland charge. He was fortunate in the quality

CASUALTIES AND THEIR TREATMENT

In a major battle the victors' losses could be negligible whereas the defeated side's casualties might be as high as 25%. Many of these took place well away from the battlefield as fugitives were hunted down. Charles II's surgeon noted how many such fugitives from the battle of Dunbar had deep gashes in their arms from protecting their heads from the sword strokes of pursuing horsemen. The victorious side invariably took everything that could be had after a battle. At Marston Moor in 1644 all the bodies on the battlefield were stripped and left lying, dead and alive alike. There were army surgeons in the 17th century but there were no anaesthetics and little understanding of the importance of sterilising equipment. Often the most seriously wounded could not reach treatment, or, as happened after defeats such as Dunbar in 1651, the surgeons fled, not unnaturally, with the rest.

A covenanter's flag dated to the late 17th century (National Museums of Scotland).

General David Leslie. He was one of the Scots' best generals, but was not given a free hand by the Committee of Estates. The result was defeat at Dunbar in 1650. Image drawn from a contemporary portrait (Shepherd).

of the men led by Alasdair MacColla, who here and elsewhere, were able to see off cavalry. Montrose certainly had ability and a flair for living dangerously. He had luck too, not least in being opposed by inexperienced troops and commanders. His reliance on Alasdair MacColla and his inability to keep his men from the chase at Tibbermore and elsewhere does, however, raise the question of just to what extent he was in control of the situation. His army fluctuated enormously in size as contingents of Highlanders came and went to their homes with booty.

Montrose's fatal weakness as a commander was the lack of attention he gave to gathering intelligence of his enemy's movements. This almost brought him to grief on several occasions before 13 September 1645, when his army, without MacColla, was easily caught and destroyed by David Leslie at Philiphaugh near Selkirk. In 1647 Leslie also drove MacColla out of his foothold in Kintyre. To many at the time it must have seemed that the scourge of Highland warfare had been banished for good.

THE DEFEAT OF THE MILITIA ARMIES

But the militia armies which were so effectively led by Leven and David Leslie, under lesser generals had been taken apart by Montrose, and were in 1650 and 1651 to be dealt blows from which they never recovered. The Scots now found themselves opposed by English parliamentary armies led by that same Oliver Cromwell who had fought alongside them at Marston Moor. In his campaign into Scotland in 1650 Cromwell was initially out-classed and out-manoeuvred by the Scots, now led in the field by David Leslie. Leslie, however, was saddled by a committee of estates (of parliament) which not only was intent on purging his army of officers and men with suspect political views but also decreed how he should conduct military affairs. The tragic result was the deliverance of an unsteady Scottish army, at Dunbar on 3 September 1650, into the hands of one of the most accomplished generals who ever set foot in this country.

David Leslie was totally exonerated of any blame for the defeat and stayed on in command, fighting a tough campaign over the winter from earthworks at Bannockburn in an attempt to keep Cromwell to the south of the Forth and Clyde. In July 1651 the battle took place which was even more of a disaster in Scottish fortunes than Dunbar. At Inverkeithing the English fought their way out of a bridge-head established on the north side of the Forth. This, however, was no excuse for the fatal decision which saw the Scots army abandon Scotland in a futile attempt to look for support in England. Leven disassociated himself from this piece of foolery and David Leslie went along most unwillingly as commander of the horse. The commander-in-chief was the inexperienced Charles II, newly crowned by the Scots and prepared to promise anything in the hope of regaining his kingdoms. The result was a complete rout at Worcester on 3 September and subjection by an English army of occupation until 1660.

Medal commemorating the Battle of Dunbar, with a bust of Cromwell and a view of the battle in the background (National Museums of Scotland).

In future, militia forces were to play second fiddle to a standing army. It is ironic that it was the rival military system of the Highlands, although thoroughly destroyed by David Leslie, which was to go on and leave its mark on British warfare for the next hundred years.

Scottish flag carried at the Battle of Dunbar in 1651 (National Museums of Scotland).

CHAPTER 8

FIGHTING FOR EMPIRE

TURNING REBELS INTO LOYAL PROFESSIONALS

In the late 17th and early 18th centuries the government had to deal with several insurrections in Scotland. As Britain flourished in the world and created a vast empire, a major strategy was to turn Scottish rebels - real, imagined and potential - into loyal, professional warriors.

There were uprisings by the more extreme covenanters of the south-west in 1666 and 1679, intent on precipitating a return to presbyterian church government, and by the Earl of Argyll in 1685, hoping to dislodge the new king, James VII (James II of England). These were all contained with relative ease by government forces. A more serious threat to orderly government was posed by the Jacobites, the supporters of the exiled James VII and the Stewart dynasty. They were mostly drawn from the Highlands, and in uprisings in 1689 and 1745, won decisive battles.

OPPOSITE: This picture, after the painting by David Morier, reconstructs the moment at Culloden in 1746 when the Highlanders attacked the left wing of Cumberland's army (National Museums of Scotland).

THE STANDING ARMY

There was obviously a need for a permanent military establishment in Scotland, and the solution from 1661 was to be a fully professional standing army. The main deterrent, now as always, to such a proposal was cost. The country had been held down very efficiently by the Cromwellian army but by 1660 this consisted of five regiments of horse, eleven regiments and one company of foot, four companies of dragoons and a train of artillery. It cost the government over twice as much a year as they raised in revenue in Scotland.

The new Scottish standing army was at first very small, consisting of no more than two troops of horse and six companies of foot, the latter being the origin of the Scots Guards. This army, however, grew and fluctuated in size according to the political panics of the day. By 1681 it was some 3,000 strong, including horse, dragoons, artillery

UNIFORMS

It was the responsibility of the officers of a regiment to supply uniforms for their men. By the 1680s the drab stone grey cloth which may have been most commonly employed was being replaced by red or scarlet (hence 'redcoats'), made up into uniforms with distinctive trimmings for each regiment. Hats varied - furred caps for the artillery and grenadiers, blue bonnets or broad brimmed felt caps for others.

The conservative General Dalyell insisted in 1684 on continuing to uniform his dragoons in grey - hence their nickname, the Scots Greys. In the 17th century only the mounted units continued to wear armour, consisting of back and breast plates and head pieces.

Viscount Dundee (1689) image drawn from a contemporary portrait (Shepherd).

and the garrisons in the castles of Edinburgh, Stirling, Dumbarton and the Bass (in the Firth of Forth). The foot included the Earl of Mar's regiment, raised in 1678, the ancestor of the Royal Scots Fusiliers. The dragoons consisted of a regiment raised in 1681, under the command of Lieutenant-General Thomas Dalyell, later to be known as the Scots Greys.

The formation of this army was due to the presence in Scotland - and the influence of - the Duke of York, Charles II's brother and future king, James VII. He had already demonstrated abilities as a commander on land and sea and had done much to reform the administration of the English navy. After he succeeded to the throne in 1685 he strengthened his Scottish army yet further.

In the autumn of 1688 King James had the entire Scottish Army of 3,763 men brought south to England to oppose the invasion led by William of Orange. Many officers in the English army had been plotting to turn themselves and their units over to William on his arrival, and it was these defections which were to lead to James' downfall. His Scottish troops, however, with few exceptions, remained loyal to him until his flight from the country, and some officers were to maintain his cause in future years. Out of a total of about 190 officers, just under half are known to have left the service or to have been dismissed in the early part of the new reign.

BONNIE DUNDEE

By far the most significant of the officers of the Scottish army who did not pay allegiance to the new king, William, was John Graham of Claverhouse, Viscount Dundee. Less than 50 years after the stirring campaigns of his distant relative, Montrose, he seemed set to emulate the marquis' achievements. James VII and II had given Dundee the task of raising forces in Scotland to help secure his return from exile. He was infamous for his cavalry actions against the covenanters in the south-west of Scotland. In the summer of 1689 he campaigned round the Highlands to try and rally the old king's supporters, but with limited success. He thus found himself at Killiecrankie late on 27 July with an army only 2,000 strong, opposing William of Orange's forces, probably twice the number, under the command of Hugh Mackay, a Scottish soldier with considerable continental experience. As with Montrose, it appears that Dundee was forced to adopt his Highlanders' tactics rather than impose his own will.

Dundee's army included a troop of about 40 horse, mostly experienced men who had served under him in the Scottish army. He also had a force of 300 Irishmen, but the main part of his army consisted of Highlanders. Dundee had apparently intended to subject them to standard military discipline and drill them as regular units, but was dissuaded from doing so by Cameron of Lochiel. They were thus drawn up at Killiecrankie in clan groups.

MacKay had marched his army northwards through the deep and narrow gorge of the River Garry, only to find Dundee's army drawn up on higher ground ahead of him. He could neither advance or retreat without exposing his troops to great danger, and had to draw out his army hurriedly, basically in the order in which it had marched. It included some experienced troops. Instead of the mixed formations with pikes and muskets of earlier times, Mackay's troops now all had muskets to which bayonets could be attached. The problem was that these were plug bayonets which fitted inside the gun barrel. The idea was that the bayonets would only be secured once the enemy was too close for further volleys of fire.

Both Dundee and Mackay needed to fight. Dundee had to gain a decisive victory to hold his army together and gain credibility for his cause. Mackay feared the approaching darkness and the risk of his lines of communication with the south being cut off. He therefore resolved to try and precipitate an attack by Dundee with his artillery. This merely consisted of three small pieces of leather artillery brought solely for their lightness, and were rendered useless when their carriages broke on the third firing.

Dundee gave the order for the attack just before sunset. His Highlanders took off their plaids and all other equipment apart from their weapons, and moved down the hillside until within a few metres of the enemy line. They fired and discarded their guns and rushed on Mackay's troops with targe and broadsword. Many of the latter never had time to secure their bayonets after firing their muskets, and the horse shied away rather than face up to

View of Killiecrankie (Caldwell).

Major General Hugh Mackay. A Scottish laird, himself, he had a distinguished career as a soldier on the Continent behind him when he faced up to Dundee at Killiecrankie in 1689; image drawn from a contemporary portrait (Shepherd).

the clansmen. Many fled without even firing a shot. The result was a total rout of the government army, Mackay only managing to lead off 600 or 700 men in the darkness. It was not until several days later that news got through that Dundee himself had been killed in the battle, shot in the initial onslaught as he rallied his troops from his horse. Without Dundee, the uprising soon fizzled out.

SERVING IN THE BRITISH ARMY

Several Scottish regiments were raised on behalf of William to counter the threat posed by Dundee, and although most were disbanded soon after the collapse of the Jacobites, it had dawned on the English government that Scotland was fertile territory for recruits for British armies. The Highlanders, had obviously performed well under Dundee, but were not yet deemed suitable material for the regiments of the line. Scottish units on the other side had also distinguished themselves, including Lord Angus' regiment (the Cameronians), raised from the covenanters who had so recently been in open rebellion. It soon confounded suspicions about its worth by repulsing the Jacobite army's attack on Dunkeld in August 1689, even though its four senior officers were killed in the fighting.

The army William sent to fight the French in Flanders was, prior to the peace of Ryswick in 1697, at times almost half composed of Scottish battalions. Andrew Fletcher of Saltoun, a member of the Scottish Parliament, could write in 1698 that:

'Seven or eight thousand of our seamen were on board the
English fleet, and two or three thousand in that of Holland:
we had twenty battalions of foot, and six squadrons of
dragoons here and in Flanders. Besides, I am credibly
informed, that every fifth man in the English forces was
either of that nation or Scots-Irish, who are a people of
the same blood with us.'

Even if there is some exaggeration in Fletcher's account he could be pardoned for also saying that Scotland had done more than her fair share in support of the English and the Dutch.

After the Union of the Parliaments of Scotland and England in 1707 the Scottish regiments became part of the new British Army. Those which were on active service in Flanders were allocated English counties as recruiting grounds and were further given a proportion of the men impressed in England under the recruiting acts. These arrangements were not a success and were soon abandoned; but although the Scottish regiments were soon recruiting largely from their own home areas they rarely returned there. Many

English regiments continued to have a high proportion of Scottish soldiers and in the 1750s were sent to Scotland to raise recruits.

THE FAILURE TO DEAL WITH HIGHLAND ARMIES

As yet there was relatively little recruitment of Highlanders into the army, although from at least 1667, it was government policy to raise companies of Highlanders to perform 'watch' or police duties in the Highlands. Their numbers grew over the years, and in 1739 these units formed the basis of the Black Watch Regiment. There was, however, still a large reservoir of manpower in the Highlands to be tapped for the Jacobite cause in 1715 and 1745. The government showed no understanding of the Highlanders' culture, or sense that their traditional form of fighting should be taken seriously.

When the Jacobites rose in 1715 command of the government forces was given to the Duke of Argyll, like Mackay before him a Highlander with considerable continental experience. But he employed the same old predictable approach – let the Highlanders attack, and if they were not seen off by a volley of gunfire, hope to take them in flank and from behind with the horse. The problem was, as at Sheriffmuir near Dunblane on 13 November, the Highlanders always broke through the opposing lines and were not readily put off by mounted troops. Only the lamentable incompetence of the Jacobite commander, the Earl of Mar, turned what should have been a great victory into a tactical defeat.

CONTAINING THE HIGHLANDS

Cromwell had controlled the Great Glen in the 1650s with forts at Inverlochy and Inverness. After his defeat at Killiecrankie in 1689 MacKay was keen to continue this policy, and in the aftermath of 1715 other barracks were built at Inversnaid, Fort William, Ruthven and Bernera. The government was also anxious to improve communications for the movement of troops and supplies, but the road building programme initiated under General Wade in 1725 was of more benefit in the '45 to the Jacobites than it was to government forces.

The ruins of Ruthven barracks, Kingussie, Inverness-shire, built in 1720. They failed to hold off a Jacobite attack in 1746 (Historic Scotland).

Prince Charles Edward Stewart, from a bronze bust dated 1746, by Jean-Baptiste Lemoyne (Shepherd).

Thirty years further on and still it seems nothing had been learnt by the government commanders sent to oppose the last of the Jacobite uprisings, occasioned by the landing in Scotland in 1745 of the Stewart heir to the throne, Prince Charles Edward, grandson of James VII. As before, the Jacobite forces were mostly recruited from the Highland clans, but now we are aware of its commanders making a conscious attempt to turn all of them into a tartan army, insisting that targes had to be carried, as if many in their ranks were unfamiliar with them or felt that their use was a thing of the past.

The government's strategy of trying to confine trouble from their rebellious clansmen to the Highlands failed miserably when they outfaced the government's army under Sir John Cope at the Corrieyairack Pass and went on to occupy Edinburgh with no serious hindrance. It was a remarkably confident Jacobite force which faced up to Cope's army again on 21 September 1745, at Prestonpans to the east of Edinburgh, both armies being then about 2,500 men strong.

A scurrilous contemporary print following the battle of Prestonpans, suggesting that Cope fled from the battlefield so fast that he was the first to bring news of his own defeat.

The battle was over in ten minutes with all of Cope's army head over heels in flight – all, that is, apart from the 500 killed and 1,400 rounded up as prisoners. The death toll would have been much worse but for the prompt action of the Jacobite commanders, especially the Earl of Perth and Lord George Murray, in reining in their men. The way was thus open for the long march south as far as Derby.

How close the uprising of 1745 actually came to succeeding is one of the great debates in Scottish history. Here we are primarily concerned with whether the Highland charge finally met its match on the field of Culloden, outside Inverness, on 16 April 1746.

94

CULLODEN

The Jacobite army at Culloden was in a far different mood from the one that had charged so eagerly at Prestonpans. It was tired and hungry, and for the first time Prince Charles had himself assumed overall command, now over officers who did not totally agree with each other on the way the prince was handling the army.

Opposing the prince was the third government army it had had to square up to, this time led by the Duke of Cumberland. He was popular with his troops and commanded respect not just as the king's son but for his undoubted bravery. At Fontenoy in 1743 he had marched his army into a barrage of deadly fire and back again in good order, leaving over 1,500 of his own dead behind him. It hardly demonstrated inspired leadership but it is unlikely that any other general at the time could command so much loyalty.

Much has been made of a novel way of drilling his men which Cumberland is credited with having introduced prior to the battle. The troops were taught to push their bayonets over the right arm against the right breast of an antagonist, and mutually to defend each other, by pushing against the man who was engaged with his right hand comrade – the point being to avoid lodging their own bayonet uselessly in an opponent's targe, but to go for the nearest, exposed right side.

At Culloden, Prince Charles had his men exposed to an effective artillery barrage for at least 15 minutes, if not much longer, before launching an all out atttack. Few of the Highlanders got as far as the enemy lines, felled by enemy fire as they struggled over unsuitable

An engraving of the Battle of Culloden, 16 April 1746 (G Williams after J Hamilton).

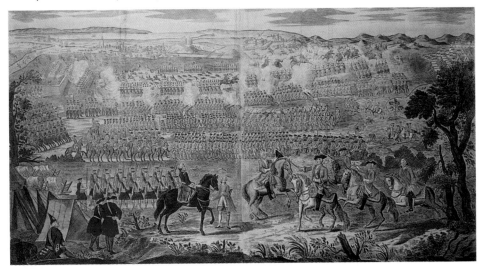

MUTINIES

ground. To avoid bogs, many of the men got so densely packed they could not fire their guns. Some, particularly the MacDonalds, may have failed to press home their attack out of pique for not being given a sufficiently honourable place in the line-up before battle. Even so, the Highlanders burst through the front line of government troops. This time, however, the second line held firm and the Highlanders were thrust back or bayoneted down. Soon the whole Jacobite army was in retreat and the prince was to show no stomach for attempting to regroup and struggle on.

Culloden was a military disaster for the Jacobites and effectively marked the end of the uprising. It was also the last occasion on which the Highland charge was seen in a major pitched battle. It cannot be concluded, however, that as a tactic it had met its match in anything that Cumberland had devised to oppose it. In other hands, at another place, there is every reason to think that it could have achieved victory over yet another conventional army.

THE ADOPTION OF A HIGHLAND STYLE

Through the '45 uprising the government had finally come to appreciate that there was a vast, potential reservoir of recruits for its own army in the Highlands, not just to fill existing units but to form new ones as well. Many, of course, argued that the best way to remove the threat of any future Jacobite disturbances was thus to deplete the islands and glens. During the Seven Years War (1756-1763), when Britain was campaigning in Europe, North America and India, 11 marching regiments were raised in Scotland, 10 of which were from the Highlands, including Montgomery's and Fraser's Highlanders, both of 1757. The latter was commanded by Simon Fraser, son of Lord Lovat, executed in 1747 for his part in the Jacobite Uprising, and notably included many officers and men who had fought for Prince Charles.

The apparent willingness of the Scots to opt for a military career is perhaps not fully understood, but some reasons can be suggested. There was the obvious lure of money and adventure for the many who were impoverished, and the numbers of these were swelled at various times by famine and the clearance of large numbers of tenants from Highland glens and the islands. There was a long tradition of bearing arms, thanks to the various uprisings and civil wars, and many in Scotland saw soldiering as an honourable profession. The Disarming Acts imposed on the population of the Highlands after the failure of the '45 not only banned weapons but Highland dress as well. Many young men must have felt this robbed them of their manhood and self-esteem. Both could be regained by joining a Highland regiment where traditional weapons and clothing were not just allowed but cherished.

Many went to serve out of ignorance, through coercion, or misguided support for clan chiefs. Men had turned out to fight for the Jacobite armies because they owed allegiance to a clan chief or because they had been called out by their landlord. The more enthusiastic Jacobite chiefs and lairds recruited clansmen and tenants ruthlessly. Sometimes the threat of a burnt house was necessary for the Jacobite cause to appear to have any relevance. In the mid and late 18th century Scottish chiefs and landlords were similarly to use their own status to raise regiments for the Hanoverian Government. Some, like Simon Fraser in 1757, and Lord MacLeod, who raised a regiment in 1777, hoped to be of sufficient service to secure the return of the lands they had forfeited as a result of the '45. Many others saw it as a means of making money – bounty money for raising the men, and more creamed off in contracts for uniforms and equipment, commissions for themselves and relatives.

Remarkably, the Highland regiments did not lose their Highland heritage, despite dilution by non-Highland blood and various changes to uniform and equipment which increasingly squeezed out their traditional garb and accoutrements. On the contrary, by the late 19th century most Lowland regiments were indistinguishable from Highland ones because they had adopted tartan trews, Highland doublets, and the same basket-hilted swords as the former. They also went into battle with their own pipers.

'The Thin Red Line' by Robert Gibb - Scottish troops (the Sutherland Highlanders) repulse a Russian charge at Balaclava in the Crimea, 1854 (by kind permission of United Distillers).

In the 19th century Scottish regiments served all over the world, policing an enormous British Empire. They fought in wars in the Crimea, Africa, India and Afghanistan. In the 20th century hundreds of thousands of Scots were enlisted into the vast armies which fought in two World Wars, and Scottish regiments remain an important part of a professional army which still serves abroad.

Despite the amalgamations of some units and the disbandment of others, along with the inevitable and ever quickening changes in uniform, equipment and methods of operation, Scottish regiments today can draw strength from their long and distinguished histories.

GLOSSARY

Aketon: quilted coat, worn by itself or under armour. Aketons were popular in the West Highlands, being represented on several grave slabs and crosses of the 14th to 16th century.

Basinet: a type of helmet, conical in shape.

Basket hilt: a type of hilt which encloses and protects the hand, commonly used on Scottish swords from the late 16th century onwards.

Battle: a main unit of a medieval army, a battalion, especially the centre unit, placed between a vanguard and a rearguard.

Bond of manrent: an agreement by which a man undertook to assist a more powerful one in return for protection.

Brigandine: jacket reinforced with metal plates riveted together.

Broadsword: a sword blade which is sharp on both edges. The term is often used for the basket-hilted swords carried by the Scots.

Buffil coat: a heavy protective coat made of leather.

Cannon: a large piece of artillery firing shot about 159mm (6 1/4 in) in diameter; used essentially for knocking down walls.

Carbine: a light gun with a shorter barrel than a *musket*, fitted with a shoulder strap for use by *dragoons*.

Castle-ward: an obligation to provide a man (men) to garrison a castle at specified times.

Chausses: mail leggings.

Chivalry: a loosely defined set of values and behaviour which the good *knight* was expected to have. They included courage, honour and courtesy, especially to the weak and to women.

Coif: a mail hood, often worn under a helmet.

Covered way: a defensive line on the outer edge of a ditch, protected by a parapet.

Culverin: an early type of long gun.

Culverin bastard: a medium-sized piece of artillery, firing shot about 97mm (4 in) in diameter.

Dirk: a type of dagger used by the Highlanders.

Donjon: a tower in a castle, larger and more secure than any other, the place where a garrison made its last stand.

Dragoon: a mounted infantryman.

Fencibles: those eligible for military service, all men aged from 16 to 60. From the 17th century fencibles, now essentially volunteer forces, have to be distinguished from the militia. Fencible regiments were raised in the 18th century during the war years, 1759-1763, 1778-1779 and 1793-1802 for the defence of Scotland while the regular troops were mostly overseas.

Firelock: an early term for a firing mechanism of a gun in which a flint strikes a spark off a steel to ignite the powder charge.

Forinsec (Scottish service): the duty placed upon landholders to do military service.

Fusee: another term for a *carbine*.

Glacis: an area of cleared ground, sloping away gently in front of a fortification, providing no cover for an enemy.

Gorget: defence for the neck, either of mail or plate.

Grenadiers: troops, first introduced into the Scottish army in 1682, armed with hand grenades and axes besides their ordinary weapons, and intended for use as storm troops.

Habergeon: coat of mail, sometimes worn over an *aketon* or under plate armour.

Hauberk: a mail coat worn by early knights.

Highland charge: the tactic employed by Highland armies, armed with *targes* and *broadswords*, in the 17th and 18th centuries. Firearms were fired and jettisoned and the enemy lines attacked at a trot.

Host: the Scottish medieval army, composed of the *fencibles*, particularly those who had to serve, on the basis of holding so much land or wealth, with appropriate equipment, food and drink. Service was for a maximum of 40 days in any one year.

Jack: jacket reinforced with metal plates.

Kettle hat: basin-shaped iron hat, normally with broad brim.

Knight: a heavily armed horseman, particularly in the 12th and 13th centuries. The term came to denote rank and be a reward for valour or service to the state.

Lance: a type of spear used by horsemen.

Man of arms: an armoured man, normally on horseback, one of the elite of a medieval army.

Militia: fighting forces raised by levying set proportions of the *fencible* men of the kingdom. Militia forces were paid and could be kept on foot for long periods of time, as in the years from 1639 to 1651. Militia regiments were also raised in the late 18th and 19th centuries.

Motte (and bailey castle): an early type of castle, with defences of earth and timber. A motte is a mound, normally artificial, with a tower or other fortifications on its summit. A **bailey** is a fortified enclosure placed adjacent to a motte.

Musket: a type of long gun. Early muskets were often so heavy that they needed to be supported on a rest when being fired.

Pike: a spear with a long shaft.

Ravelin: a detached triangular fortification built in front of a castle or fort.

Regiment: a unit of men theoretically, if rarely, 1,000 strong, commanded by a colonel.

Sallet: type of helmet with round skull, often extending into a point at the back as a protection for the neck. Some had visors and face defences.

Schiltrom: a defensive arrangement for large units of spearmen fighting on foot, providing protection from attack on all sides.

Serjeant: a mounted man less completely armed than a knight.

Slogad: the Gaelic term for the gathering together of the host or army for a military campaign.

Splint: plate defence for either an arm or a leg.

Surcoat: a cloth coat worn over armour.

Targe/target: a circular shield of wood covered with leather. It is a medieval type, but continued in use amongst the Highlanders into the 18th century.

Trace italienne: the term used for fortifications, first fully developed in Italy in the early 16th century, with an earthwork component and careful provision for flanking gunfire, principally with angular bastions, either pentagonal in shape, or like arrowheads.

Wapinschawing: meetings for checking the arms and armour of the *fencibles* and their ability to perform military service. They were normally convened by the sheriffs and other local royal officials.

INDEX

FURTHER READING

There are several popular works on battles and battlefield sites. There is detailed coverage of Scottish ones in D Smurthwaite, *The Ordnance Survey Complete Guide to the Battlefields of Britain* (1984). P Marren's *Grampian Battlefields* (1990) is a particularly good regional guide.

G W S Barrow's *Robert Bruce* (1976) remains the best biography of Scotland's greatest king, and should be read for its account of Willian Wallace and the Wars of Independence as well. Alexander Leslie is dealt with by C S Terry, *The Life and Campaigns of Alexander Leslie, First Earl of Leven* (1899). D Stevenson, in his *Alasdair MacColla and the Highland Problem in the 17th Century* (1980) focuses attention on Montrose's lieutenant rather than Montrose himself, and develops the theme of the Highland Charge.

The campaigning of the Jacobite army in the '45 is well dealt with by K Tomasson and F Buist, *Battles of the '45* (1962). The same battles are viewed from the Hanoverian point of view in W A Speck's *The Butcher. The Duke of Cumberland and the Suppression of the '45* (1981). S Wood gives a general account of Scottish armed forces from the 17th century to the present day in *The Scottish Soldier* (1987).

For Scottish arms and armour see D H Caldwell, *The Scottish Armoury* (1979). C J Tabraham provides an introduction to Scotland's castles in *Scottish Castles and Fortifications* (1986) and many of the castles in the care of Historic Scotland have informative guide books.

There are several good histories of Scotland in print which deal with warfare to a greater or lesser extent. *The Edinburgh History of Scotland* in four volumes, by A A M Duncan, R Nicholson, G Donaldson and W Ferguson is particularly useful for the serious scholar, not only for its detailed treatment of important events but for the information it provides on original sources.

SELECTIVE LIST OF SITES TO VISIT

Chapter 1
Aberlemno cross-slab (Aberlemno Kirkyard), Angus (Historic Scotland)
Antonine Wall (in particular Croy Hill, near Glasgow) (Historic Scotland)
Dunadd Fort, Argyll (Historic Scotland)
Museum of Scotland, Edinburgh, for weapons, sculpture, etc

Chapter 2
Battle of Largs Monument, Largs, Ayrshire
Bothwell Castle, Lanarkshire (Historic Scotland)
Caerlaverock Castle, Dumfries-shire (Historic Scotland)
Duffus Castle, Moray
Kildrummy Castle, Aberdeenshire (Historic Scotland)

Chapter 3
Bannockburn Visitor Centre, Bannockburn, Stirling (National Trust for Scotland)
Wallace Monument, Stirling

Chapter 4
Lochleven Castle, Kinross (Historic Scotland)
Edinburgh Castle, for Mons Meg (Historic Scotland)

Threave Castle, Kirkcudbrightshire (Historic Scotland)
Ravenscraig Castle, Dysart, Fife (Historic Scotland)

Chapter 6
Eyemouth Fort, Eyemouth, Berwickshire
St Andrews Castle, Fife (Historic Scotland)
Tantallon Castle, East Lothian (Historic Scotland)

Chapter 7
Museum of Scotland, Edinburgh, for weapons, etc

Chapter 8
Culloden Battlefield and Visitor Centre, Inverness-shire (National Trust for Scotland)
Duns Law, Duns castle, Berwickshire (Historic Scotland)
Fort George, Inverness-shire (Historic Scotland)
Killiecrankie Battlefield and Visitor Centre, Perthshire (National Trust for Scotland)
Scottish United Services Museum, Edinburgh Castle

Printed in Scotland for The Stationery Office Limited
J50432, C30, 6/98, CCN 056901.